PENAL POPULISM

JOHN PRATT

Routledge
Taylor & Francis Group

LONDON AND NEW YORK

First published 2007
by Routledge
2 Park Square, Milton Park, Abingdon, Oxon OX14 4RN

Simultaneously published in the USA and Canada
by Routledge
270 Madison Ave, New York, NY 10016

Routledge is an imprint of the Taylor & Francis Group, an informa business

© 2007 John Pratt

Typeset in Garamond 3 by RefineCatch Limited, Bungay, Suffolk
Printed and bound in Great Britain by
TJ International Ltd, Padstow, Cornwall

British Library Cataloguing in Publication Data
A catalogue record for this book is available from the British Library

Library of Congress Cataloging in Publication Data
Pratt, John.
    Penal populism: key ideas in criminology / John Pratt.
        p. cm.
    Includes bibliographical references and index.
    ISBN 0–415–38509–1 (hardcover: alk. paper) — ISBN 0–415–38508–3
(softcover: alk. paper) 1. Sentences (Criminal procedure)—Public opinion.
2. Punishment—Public opinion. 3. Criminal justice, Administration of—
Public opinion. 4. Crime—Government policy—Public opinion.
5. Populism. I. Title.

HV8708.P44 2007
364.6—dc22   2006019040

ISBN10: 0–415–38509–1 (hbk)
ISBN10: 0–415–38508–3 (pbk)
ISBN10: 0–203–96367–9 (ebk)

ISBN13: 978–0–415–38509–1 (hbk)
ISBN13: 978–0–415–38508–4 (pbk)
ISBN13: 978–0–203–96367–8 (ebk)

PENAL POPULISM

Following the lead of the USA, prison rates in many Western countries have soared while crime rates have been declining. Governments have developed penal policies in line with the sentiments and aspirations of the general public rather than their own bureaucratic organizations. This penal populism has led to much stronger relationships between politicians and those who claim to speak for the public – such as anti-crime social movements, talk-back radio hosts, and victims' rights lobbyists.

This book argues that governments have increasingly allowed penal populism to impact on policy development and that there has been less reliance on the expertise of civil servants and academics. This fascinating book shows that the roots of penal populism lie in the collapse of trust in the modern institutions of government, the decline of deference and the growth of ontological insecurity, along with new media technologies helping to spread it. It has had most influence in the development of policy on sex offenders, youth crime, persistent criminals and 'incivilities', and anti-social behaviour. Nonetheless, it is by no means an inevitable phenomenon in modern penal systems – there are societies with strong central bureaucracies which have blocked it. There are also limits to penal populism – the public do not have an insatiable appetite for punishment – and there has been resistance to it from judges, lawyers, academics and the restorative justice movement.

The book is a fascinating exposé of current crime policy development and poses important questions for the future. It will be essential reading for students, researchers and professionals working in criminology and crime policy.

John Pratt is Professor of Criminology at the Institute of Criminology, Victoria University of Wellington. He has published extensively on the history and sociology of punishment, including *Punishment in a Perfect Society* (1992), *Governing the Dangerous* (1997), *Dangerous Offenders: Punishment and Social Order* (2000, joint editor), *Punishment and Civilization* (2002), *Crime, Truth and Justice* (2003, joint editor) and *The New Punitiveness* (2005, co-editor).

KEY IDEAS IN CRIMINOLOGY

Series Editor: TIM NEWBURN, Mannheim Centre for Criminology, London School of Economics

Key Ideas in Criminology explores the major concepts, issues, debates and controversies in criminology. The series aims to provide authoritative essays on central topics within the broader area of criminology. Each book adopts a strong individual 'line', constituting original essays rather than literature surveys, and offer lively and agenda setting treatments of their subject matter.

These books will appeal to students, teachers and researchers in criminology, sociology, social policy, cultural studies, law and political science.

Series editor Tim Newburn is Professor of Criminology and Social Policy, Director of the Mannheim Centre for Criminology, London School of Economics and President of the British Society of Criminology. He has written and researched widely on issues of crime and justice.

Forthcoming in the series:

Rehabilitation
TONY WARD AND
SHADD MARUNA

Security
LUCIA ZEDNER

Surveillance
BENJAMIN GOOLD

Feminist Criminology
CLAIRE RENZETTI

Victims
PAUL ROCK

Policing
MICHAEL KEMPA AND
CLIFFORD SHEARING

For Isabella, as always

'Democracy which began by liberating men politically has developed a dangerous tendency to enslave him through the tyranny of majorities and the deadly power of their opinion.'

– Ludwig Lewisohn, *The Modern Drama*, p. 17

CONTENTS

ACKNOWLEDGEMENTS

I am delighted to be able to make this contribution to the *Routledge Key Ideas in Criminology* series. My interest in penal populism began while I was writing a previous book, *Punishment and Civilization*: it was obviously becoming an important new dynamic in penal development. It was then given extra stimulation by the force it began to have in New Zealand, where I live, and, with a graduate student, Marie Clark, I began to explore its local causes and consequences and published in *Punishment and Society*. The opportunity to put these explorations on a much bigger canvas came about through initial conversations with Philip Smith and encouragement from the series editor, Tim Newburn. I am grateful for the interest and support I have since received from Gerhard Boomgaarden and Constance Sutherland at Routledge.

While the book was being written, my research assistant, Anne Holland, was remarkably diligent and painstaking and I am most grateful to her for her help. Janet Chan, Tapio Lappi-Seppälä, Tim Newburn and Mick Ryan kindly commented on earlier drafts of four of the chapters. Most of the data on prison trends has been taken from the outstanding website of the International Centre for Prison Studies, Kings

College, London University. My work benefited greatly from a visit as a Visiting Professor to the Law Faculty of the University of Helsinki in 2006 and I would like to thank the Dean of the Faculty, Jukka Kekkonen, for arranging this. I would also like to thank the group of people who at various times supplied me with references, sent me papers, patiently dealt with my enquiries, gave me ideas and made suggestions. These are: Maria Archimanditrou, David Brown, Pat Carlen, Mick Cavadino, Kathy Daly, Tony Doob, Roger Grimshaw, Bryan Hogeveen, Katja Franko-Aas, Eric Janus, Raimo Lahti, Dag Leonardsen, Ian Loader, Paul Mazerolle, Mike Nellis, Pat O'Malley, Russell Smandych, Peter Squires, Henrik Tham, Terry Thomas, Renee van Swaningen and Frank Zimring. I have been very fortunate to have enjoyed the support and forbearance of Anna Chang while working on this project. Finally, I would like to thank my daughter Isabella and my dog Suzie for being themselves.

INTRODUCTION

A leading article in *The Guardian* (1 November 2001: 8)
noted that the Lord Chief Justice, the Chief Inspector
of Prisons and the Director General of Prisons had all
complained about the growth of imprisonment in Britain.
However, 'the response was abysmal. True to tradition, both
major parties indulged in a round of penal populism.'
Shortly afterwards, the same paper reported that 'scared
of being seen to be weak on law 'n' order, [the Home
Secretary has] opted for penal populism. In a system which
already imprisoned more people than the most hardline
states . . . he [has] opted to tighten the screw further' (*The
Guardian* 12 December 2001: 18). *The Scotsman* (16 May
2005: 3) reported that Scotland's Young Thinker of the Year
was interested in penal reform. She had said in a speech
acknowledging her award that 'it appears to be a vote winner to say that a party will be tough on crime, but an urgent
change of direction away from this "penal populism" is
required.'

At the opposite end of the globe, the *Adelaide Review*
(28 September 2004: 6) noted that the South Australia
Labour Government had 'wholeheartedly embraced "penal

populism", largely through an aggressive policy of longer sentences.' Writing in the *Sydney Morning Herald* (13 November 2003: 10), a former Western Australia Premier complained that 'too many politicians have been seduced into implementing costly and ineffective policies; they have embraced penal populism, enacting policies which are based primarily on their anticipated popularity rather than their effectiveness.' Similarly, *The Australian* (30 December 2005: 4) stated that '[the] Western Australia Attorney-General has denied the Government's approach to justice issues amounts to little more than "penal populism" and has rejected claims it treated the state's parole board as a political football.' It must be quite rare for an important criminological concept to find its way into popular journalism and everyday discourse. Nonetheless, as we can see from this range of reports, this is what has happened to penal populism.

It is a concept with a short history. Its origins lie in the work of Sir Anthony Bottoms (1995) who coined the term 'populist punitiveness' to describe one of the four main influences which he saw at work on contemporary criminal justice and penal systems in modern society. As such, it was 'intended to convey the notion of politicians tapping into and using for their own purposes, what they believe to be the public's generally punitive stance' (Bottoms 1995: 40). Thereafter, populist influences on penal policy and thought have been detected by numerous other scholars in a broad range of countries – all the way from Sweden (Tham 2001) to New Zealand (Pratt and Clark 2005) in fact. At some point, the expression 'populist punitiveness' largely gave way to 'penal populism' – Newburn (1997) being one of the first to use this latter terminology – as the means to identify these tendencies. However, for all intents and purposes, it would seem that those who use these different terms are writing about the same events, which normally have the identifying features outlined in the above newspaper reports.

For example, very similar to Bottoms (1995), Roberts *et al.* (2003: 5, my italics) state that '*penal populists allow the electoral advantage of a policy to take precedence over its penal effectiveness*. In short, penal populism consists of the pursuit of a set of penal policies to win votes rather than to reduce crime or to promote justice.'

The argument developed in this book, however, is that penal populism should not be understood merely in terms of local political opportunism, which 'buys' electoral popularity by cynically increasing levels of penal severity because it is thought that there is public support for this, irrespective of crime trends. Obviously, politicians do exploit these opportunities, but penal populism itself represents much more than this. As Chapter 1 explains, it is the product of deep social and cultural changes which began in the 1970s and which now extend across much of modern society. The rise of penal populism is the reflection of a fundamental shift in the axis of contemporary penal power brought about by these changes, even if the extent of the shift differs from society to society, depending on their local impact. Beginning around the mid 1980s, but becoming a more clearly recognizable force in the early 1990s and then quickly gathering pace thereafter, what this has led to is a much stronger resonance between governments and various extra-establishment individuals, groups and organizations which claim to speak on behalf of 'the people' in relation to the general development of penal policy; as this has happened, establishment advisers to governments have increasingly had to share the previously exclusive role they enjoyed with these new forces; indeed, they are sometimes sidelined or ignored altogether as policy is developed. The consequences of penal populism are thus more far reaching than politicians simply 'tapping' into the public mood as and when it suits them. It is not something they can simply turn off at will. Because of the power realignment that penal populism represents, they may be just as likely to lose control of it as to be able to manipulate it for their own purposes.

What are, though, these social and cultural changes that lie behind the rise of penal populism? Chapter 2 argues that its rise has been only tangentially linked to crime levels, in so far as perceptions of rising crime become one contributor – probably one of the most visible – to the sense that modern society is changing in ways that are threatening and unwanted by many. More generally, it is as if the pillars on which the security and stability of modern life had been built are fragmenting, while at the same time the authority of the state and its representatives has been declining. This has been because of disillusionment with existing political processes and declines in deference to elite opinion-formers. This can then lead to a dramatic redrawing of the processes of government and democracy, with the effect that 'people are less and less prepared to leave questions, including difficult *penal* questions to their masters' (Ryan 2004: 9). Instead, they now insist on having some sort of 'say' in this themselves; or they give their support to populist organizations or politicians who seem to be speaking for them and offering simple, understandable solutions to crime and other problems. By so doing, populists hold out promises of being able to repair the declines in authority and social order, thereby providing a vision of the future that seems less fraught with menace and uncertainty.

It is also clear, though, that perceptions about crime and the relationship these then have to penal populism have been influenced by the mass media and the impact of new information technology. Chapter 3 argues that the media can have the effect of both shaping, solidifying and directing public sentiment and opinion on crime and punishment, while simultaneously reflecting it back as the authentic voice(s) of ordinary people (Hall 1979). At the same time, the new technology compresses the news media into an ever-more simplistic form, so that it becomes something between information and entertainment. This makes it more susceptible to commonsensical populist accounts and explanations at the expense of the more elaborate, involved and thereby indigestible opinions of elitist experts. Indeed, the channels of influence and authority of the latter have been steadily retracting as this has happened. In contrast, the public at large are regularly invited to 'have their say', to quote the phrase regularly thrown out by BBC newsreaders to their audience: to put forward their own point of view about the news by e-mail or fax, put forward their own point of view to talk-back radio, even help to make the news itself by transmitting photographs via their mobile phones 'as news breaks' to television companies, or be interviewed themselves as on the spot witnesses through the same channel of communication. Overall, decisions about reporting, commenting, even deciding what actually constitutes the news have become much more democratized and diversified. And as part of this process, there is a much greater credence given to the accounts of ordinary individuals rather than to elite opinion. Those of the victims of crime are now likely to outweigh the more abstract analytical comments of experts: with concomitant effects on the way in which the news is reported and understood and penal populism fuelled.

What has this actually meant, though, in terms of the development of crime control policy? One thing is clear: it has not led to the growth of some all-embracing 'war on crime', on all crime, big or small, notwithstanding some of the wilder aspirations and expectations that emanate from populist politicians or self-acclaimed spokespeople of the public from time to time. Instead, as is explained in Chapter 4, populist responses to crime are strongest and would seem most likely to influence policy when they are presaged around a common enemy, a group of criminals who seem utterly different from the rest of the population, and whose presence when it comes to light unites the rest of the community in outrage against them: a common enemy whose activities only add to the pervading sense of anxiety and tension characteristic of everyday life in late modernity (Giddens 1990) – hence concerted measures against sex offenders, particularly child sex offenders. Or around those who, through their conduct, endanger the *precarious* quality of life that most of us have had to strive and struggle for (in the market-driven societies that many Western countries have become since the 1970s, it is no longer provided for us as of right by the state): in these respects, recidivist offenders, juveniles who seem beyond the law and even minor criminality, such as 'anti-social behaviour' in Britain, have all come under the populist spotlight.

Nonetheless, penal populism is not the only force at work on contemporary penal strategy and thought. Bottoms (1995) identified three others in competition with it: just deserts/human rights; managerialism and invocations of 'community'. Chapter 5 reviews the positioning of these forces a decade or so later, alongside two new ones that have since emerged: incapacitatory and restorative penalties. In contrast to the limited possibilities that Bottoms then identified for populist punitiveness/penal populism, I argue that this has since become one of the most significant of these influences – sometimes at the expense of these others, sometimes in association with them. However, this does not mean that its growth is boundless once it is able to put down roots in a given jurisdiction. There are in-built defences that can contest and restrict it. Furthermore, the resources that are needed to fuel its demands also have their limits.

Is it the case, though, given that its causes are related to deep structural change across modern society rather than the duplicities of individual politicians, that penal populism is an inevitable characteristic of late modernity? As Chapter 6 illustrates, it is not inevitable: there are modern societies (illustrative reference is made to Canada, Germany and Finland) where these changes have yet to take hold, or where social arrangements have acted as barriers which can be successfully placed in front of it: although these barriers are not innate characteristics of these societies. If they come down, or the social arrangements that built them are changed so that gaps appear in them, then this is likely to provide the opportunities for penal populism to make its entrance. This does not then mean, though, that there are no possibilities of resistance to this phenomenon once it does take hold, with the potential it then has to 'overwhelm and undermine the institutional architecture of liberal democracy' (Loader 2005: 23). But this of necessity also means engaging with the new terms of penal debate that these changes have produced.

Finally, the book analyses penal populism *as a general phenomenon* and the consequences and implications that this then has for penal development in modern society as a whole, rather than analysing its characteristics and dynamics in any one particular society. At the same time, specific examples are given from those countries where it has been particularly influential, and from those countries which have proved more resistant to it.

1

WHAT IS PENAL POPULISM?

Despite widespread usage of the term 'penal populism' in much analytical work on contemporary punishment, what populism *might actually be* has to date received very little consideration, as both Sparks (2001) and Matthews (2005) have observed. Instead, it is usually treated as a commonsense given, a label to attach to politicians who devise punitive penal policies that seem to be in any way 'popular' with the general public. However, penal populism is both a more complex issue than is acknowledged in those commentaries in which it is seen in this rather limited way; and more structurally embedded, representing a major shift in the configuration of penal power in modern society, rather than something within the purview of politicians to tinker with as they please. This becomes clear when we grasp the sociological significance of populism itself. From there, we can then assess what it is that is specifically populist about *penal* populism, and consider the implications and consequences that then follow from these identifying parameters.

POPULISM

In one of the first examinations of the term, Shils (1956: 100–1, my italics) observed that 'populism exists wherever there is an ideology of popular *resentment* against the order imposed on society by a long established, differential ruling class which is believed to have a monopoly of power, property, breeding and fortune.' Similarly Canovan (1981: 9, my italics) noted that populism should be understood as a 'particular kind of political phenomenon where the *tensions* between the elite and the grass roots loom large.' What they are saying, then, is that populism represents in various guises the moods, sentiments and voices of *significant and distinct segments of the public*: not public opinion in general, but instead those segments which feel that they have been ignored by governments, unlike more favoured but less deserving groups; those segments which feel they have been disenfranchised in some way or other by the trajectory of government policy which seems to benefit less worthy others but not them. It speaks specifically *for* this group who feel they have been 'left out' and is thus a reflection of their sense of alienation and dissatisfaction.

By corollary, it also speaks out *against* those other sectors of society which it judges to have been complicit in allowing this lack of representation to occur, in engineering this marginalization and disenfranchisement of 'ordinary people' who have usually made no claims on the state other than to be allowed to live their lives as such. Those thought to be responsible for this are to be found in the government's own bureaucratic organizations; sometimes the entire parliamentary process which is seen as self-serving rather than public serving; sometimes various elite groups outside of government but which periodically advise it – academics, the judiciary, some sections of the media, all thought to be out of touch with the everyday realities and concerns of the public at large. Taken together, they represent a loose fitting coalition of forces which make up 'the establishment'. As, such, rather than populism merely being a device to bring political popularity, its central aim is 'to inject the will of the people into the democratic decision-making process' (de Raadt *et al.* 2004: 3), or at least the will of those people whom governments are thought to have previously taken for granted and ignored. To do this, it also has to break down those barriers represented by the establishment that might prevent this from happening.

By the same token, in a bid to re-establish their credentials with this diffuse but voluble constituency, populist politicians in mainstream political parties choose to distance themselves from their own traditional constituencies of support (indeed, these are often turned into implacable enemies) and demonstrate that they are on the side of 'the people' rather than vested interest groups within their own parties. In Britain, we saw this in relation to the Conservative Party during the Thatcher era and we have also seen it, from the early 1990s, with New Labour. In both cases, to win over previously unsympathetic sections of the electorate, their leaders spoke of the aspirations of 'ordinary people' over the heads of 'One Nation' Tory 'grandees' in the first example, trade unions in the second.

However, it would also seem that the gulf that has opened up between mainstream politics and this sizeable if diffuse constituency of dissatisfaction and disenchantment can often no longer be bridged simply by representatives of mainstream politics making overtures to it. Instead, this constituency has played an important role in the development of a new politics. We see this reflected in two ways. First, the development of new political parties that are *specifically* populist, campaigning for election on such matters as immigration and asylum seekers, while often also promising to reduce the size of the state by cutting down the privileges of tax-payer-funded bureaucrats and civil servants. In Western Europe,[1] for example, there has been the rise of the Austrian Freedom Party; in the Netherlands, Lijst Pim Fortuyn; in Denmark, the Danish People's Party; in Belgium, Vlaams Block; the Swiss People's Party in Switzerland; New Democracy in Sweden; the Progress Party in Norway. With the exception of these last two examples, which remained peripheral players in their respective body politic (Anderson 1996, Rydgren 2002), these new parties have achieved considerable electoral success, if mercurial and contingent, even being voted into government in the case of the Austrian and Dutch examples, and becoming part of a ruling Conservative coalition in the Danish one. In Australia, there has been the rise of the One Nation Party, with its strong anti-immigration, anti-establishment platform, as with its New Zealand counterpart New Zealand First. While the former enjoyed most of its success at state rather than federal levels of government, the latter has twice been a junior partner in governing coalitions since its formation in 1992. The successes of these new parties can also shift the policy boundaries of mainstream parties. These may be compelled to incorporate some elements of populism to ward off defections to their new rivals.

Second, there has been the growth of more direct democracy initiatives, such as referenda and citizen-based ballots. These are seen as providing the opportunity for more authentic expressions of public will, rather than allowing this to be determined by governments and their advisers. In addition, there has been growing support for electoral systems based on proportional representation rather than 'first past the post' winner takes all. This, it is claimed, ensures that parliaments will be more representative of the general public. New Zealand thus changed its electoral process in this way in 1993, as well as introducing provision for non-binding citizens' initiated referenda at the same time.

The net result of both dimensions of this new politics has been the growth of a much stronger resonance between populist politicians and extra-establishment forces – pressure groups, citizens' rights advocates, talk-back radio hosts and callers and so on – all of whom claim to speak on behalf of or represent the public at large. Populist politicians look to these groups not only for support, but also for prompts and indicators for policy development and initiatives. In such ways, then, populism has been able to shift the terms of political debate. It has moved away from consensus politics where the values and aspirations of the establishment were of central influence, to a politics that is more divisive and sectarian, but which is also more in tune with the ideas and expectations of the public at large.

PENAL POPULISM

Against this backcloth, *penal* populism speaks to the way in which criminals and prisoners are thought to have been favoured at the expense of crime victims in particular and the law-abiding public in general. It feeds on expressions of anger, disenchantment and disillusionment with the *criminal justice* establishment. It holds this responsible for what seems to have been the insidious inversion of commonsensical priorities: protecting the well-being and security of law-abiding 'ordinary people', punishing those whose crimes jeopardize this. And as with populism itself, penal populism usually takes the form of 'feelings and intuitions' (Sparks 2000) rather than some more quantifiable indicator: for example, expressions of everyday talk between citizens which revolves around concerns and anxieties about crime and disorder (see Taylor 1995, Taylor *et al*. 1996, Girling *et al*. 2000); anger and concern about these matters volubly expressed in the media – not simply the national press or broadcasters (many of which are anyway thought to be too closely aligned to the not to be trusted establishment) but the popular press in particular: thus in Britain, *The Sun, Daily Mirror* and *News of the World* 'red top' newspapers have been used to launch new crime control initiatives by the New Labour Government (see Ryan 2004, Squires and Stephen 2005, Crawford 2006 for examples); and a variety of new information and media outlets which allow the voices of the general public a much more direct airing – local newspapers and news sheets (Taylor 1995), talk-back radio and reality television. At the same time, while penal populism is clearly something more than public opinion *per se* (Bottoms 1995: 40), it is not averse to using evidence from such surveys to bolster the claims it makes.

Furthermore, penal populism feeds on division and dissent rather than consensus. In these respects, it is as if a huge gulf now exists between the penal expectations of the public at large and the policies and practices of the criminal justice authorities. The focus groups whom Hough (1996: 195) surveyed thought that 'sentencers were too old, remote and out of touch – "belonging to an elite class", "from another planet", "in cloud cuckoo land", "giving out ridiculous sentences and making ridiculous statements" '; views which have been subsequently confirmed in British crime surveys (Hough 1998, Mattinson and Mirrlees-Black 2000). In the United States, public confidence in the criminal justice system was third lowest of 14 institutions of government surveyed (Hough and Roberts 2004: 30). Indeed, as penal populism has become more strident, the residual conventions and protocols that had hitherto protected such elite groups from public scrutiny and criticism have been regularly breached. Thus Roberts *et al.* (2003: 54) note that:

> The traditional separation of powers between parliament and the executive and the judiciary that is a hallmark of the Westminster system of government appears to be breaking

down . . . The 1990s saw increasing public criticism from populist politicians regarding the courts, tribunals and individual
judges.

When penal populism has been influential, though, such
developments are to be expected. They become a way of
ensuring that policy in this sphere is more reflective of
the public will than the values of the criminal justice
establishment.

As such, in a defining moment in the development of
penal populism in Britain, Home Secretary Michael Howard
famously proclaimed in 1993 that 'prison works: this may
mean that more people will go to prison. I do not flinch from
that. We shall no longer judge the success of our system
of justice by a fall in the prison population' (quoted by
Cavadino and Dignan 2002: 34). Here, he was signalling his
intention to reverse the long-held expectations of the penal
establishment (Windlesham 1998, Loader 2005) that penal
policy must have a reduction of the prison population as its
primary purpose, since high levels of imprisonment were *ipso
facto* an unwelcome stain on the texture of any country which
professed to belong to the civilized world. In effect, what
Howard was saying was that a rise in the prison population
would work in so far as criminals would be kept off the
streets. He was completely ignoring the well-known argument – at least in establishment circles – that by sending
them to prison the vast majority would come out much
worse human beings and much more committed to crime.
Instead, he was signalling to the general public that their
immediate concerns for protection and security were more
central to his thinking.

Then, in 1995, in a speech to the Police Superintendents'
Association, he stated that 'there is still public dismay over
sentencing' (quoted by Dunbar and Langdon 1998: 121).
Here was another populist signal. Now sentencing would no

longer be allowed to remain the exclusive property of the judiciary with inbuilt inoculation against public scrutiny. Furthermore, this public dismay had to be acted on: if not by the judiciary then by politicians such as himself, who *were* in tune with rightful public aspirations and who *were* prepared to put these into law to defeat judicial resistance to them. At that time, such intents fractured whatever consensus may have then been in existence between the government and its senior judges. Whether this was done deliberately, or whether short term political expediency was all Howard was interested in,[2] without any consideration for the broader consequences, these judges, remarkably, given their own hierarchical and privileged lineage, now found themselves in the position of being some of the strongest critics of Conservative Party penal policy. Hence Lord Chief Justice Taylor's response to the Conservative Government's *Protecting the Public* White Paper (Home Office 1996), designed to put the 'prison works' philosophy into strategic effect: 'I venture to suggest that never in the history of our criminal law have such far reaching proposals been put forward on the strength of such flimsy and dubious evidence' (House of Lords [1996] 572, col. 1025). In relation to the mandatory sentencing proposals in the same document, Master of the Rolls Lord Donaldson claimed that the White Paper gave 'a message loud and clear that the judges are not to be trusted' (ibid., col. 1049). He was right. Howard was indicating that he trusted 'the people', not this out of touch elite.

Similarly in New Zealand, the Labour Justice Minister, shortly after his party came to power in 1999, warned judges that they risked losing their discretionary sentencing powers if they did not impose longer prison sentences: 'public opinion does not take kindly to being ignored, particularly when there is a suspicion it is being dismissed arrogantly' (*The Press* 26 February 2000: 1). The Labour Government then set up a Judicial Complaints Process in 2001 'to oversee the appointment, monitoring and disciplining of judges. [The Justice Minister] said "a worryingly large number of people no longer have full confidence in the justice system" ' (*The Dominion* 26 February 2000: 3). There has since been only one complaint made to it – and that was unsuccessful. However, it had a symbolic rather than strategic importance. It was clearly a gesture from the Labour Government informing judges that they were mere civil servants, not some august body above the rest of the population, and could ultimately be dismissed if the public were not satisfied with their performance.

There have also been regular attacks, usually in the form of moral outrage and condemnation rather than reasoned argument, against those other elite individuals or groups who deign to proffer opinions in conflict with what is thought to be the prevailing mood of the public, or at least perceptions of this. For example, in Australia, a leading article in the Sydney *Daily Telegraph* (6 September 2002: 6) proclaimed that:

> It is no overstatement to suggest that, on sentencing, it has been The People versus The Law Society, the Council for Civil Liberties, a handful of eminent jurists and a few chin-scratchers in tweed jackets from the University of New South Wales.[3]

No longer regarded as privileged practitioners or commentators in whose expertise lies the answer to crime problems, such elites are seen as standing in the way of the more legitimate demands of the public at large. Similarly, in the immediate aftermath of the New Zealand general election of 2002 where law and order had been a particularly prominent issue, Governor General and former High Court Judge Dame Silvia Cartwright was angrily criticized by prominent opposition MPs when she challenged populist assumptions by making the comment 'prisons don't work' while opening the Crime and Justice Research Centre at Victoria University (Pratt and Clark 2005).

By privileging the penal expectations of the public over those of the criminal justice establishment, it follows that there is a commonsensical anti-intellectual nature to penal populism – in line with what Canovan (1999: 3–5) has described as being one of the attributes of populism in general: 'in employing a "tabloid" rhetorical style of communication that bears simplicity and directness, populism seeks to step over formal political institutions to become, ultimately, of the people but not of the system.' In these respects, anecdote and personal experience are better able to convey the authenticity of crime experiences than mere statistics. As a result, populist debate about crime and punishment revolves more around the emotion that such representations invoke rather than rational, considered judgement. Take, for example, the speech made in New Zealand by Dr Don Brash, Leader of the Opposition National Party, when introducing its law and order policy in 2004:

> I don't intend to recite a lot of statistics to make my case. *We all know* that New Zealand has a terrible record. It is in front of us each day ... Every day the media carry stories of horrendous crimes – appalling family violence, resulting in death and disfigurement for women and children; random killings by drug-crazed criminals out on parole; brutal muggings of young tourists visiting our country; dangerous and often drunk drivers, many with numerous driving convictions, killing people on the roads.
>
> (Brash 2004: 1, my italics)

The fact that recorded crime had already been in decline in this country for some ten years became irrelevant to his discourse.[4] Crime levels were to be judged on the basis of 'what we all know' rather than any such abstract quantifications. It was this that determined its reality, not statistical detail.

Furthermore, to emphasize the way in which the criminal justice establishment is supposed to have privileged the interests of the criminal over those of victims and the rest of the law-abiding community, victimization assumes an iconic status in populist discourse. As David Garland (2001: 144) has written:

> The symbolic figure of the victim has taken on a life of its own, and plays a key role in political and policy argument. The crime victim is no longer represented as an unfortunate citizen who has been on the receiving end of a criminal harm. His or her concerns are no longer subsumed within 'the public interest' that guides prosecution and penal decisions. Instead, the crime victim is now, in a certain sense, a representative character whose experience is assumed to be common and collective, rather than individual and atypical.

Indeed, the way in which particular laws have been named after crime victims becomes a way of honouring their loss while also memorializing them through the protection that the legislation they have inspired provides for potential victims in the future. This breaks through the cold anonymity of criminal justice procedure and captures the emotive force that victimization brings with it: the New Jersey Megan's Law in 1994; the 1994 Jacob Wetterling Act; Jessica's Law, or the 2005 California Sexual Predator Punishment and Control Act; Christopher's Law in 2001, more formally known as the Ontario Sex Offender Registry Law; proposals for 'Sarah's Law' in Britain in 2000 – all named after a child who had been sexually assaulted and murdered.

In these respects, victims' voices, or the voices of those who claim (often with no authority at all to do so) to speak on their behalf has been given an authenticity and validity in relation to the development of crime control policies, while the authority and influence of the criminal justice expert has been decried and reduced. For example, after the murder of his 18-year-old daughter in 1992 in Fresno, California, Mike Reynolds organized and campaigned for a three strikes law in that state which, uniquely among such laws in America, mandates a 25 year or life term for *any* felony, not just a serious felony. On the arrest of the accomplice to this (the murderer had died in a shootout with the police), he pointed out that 'the State of California was the one unindicted per-petrator in [his] daughter's murder' (quoted by Domanick 2004: 68). In other words, because of their early release from prison policy which set free recidivists like the one who murdered her, the state authorities were just as culpable as those who committed the crime itself. After the success of his ballot (a 67 percent vote in favour), the three strikes law came into effect without ever being referred for civil service or academic advice (Zimring 1996), so politicized had the issues associated with it become. To have backed away from its remarkable content, the Governor of California would not only have appeared fatally weak on crime, he would also have impugned the authenticity of Reynolds' own experi-ence as the father of a crime victim. Instead, after the bill had been passed into law, the Governor told Reynolds that it would be 'the most meaningful possible memorial to your own lovely daughter . . . and to all the children of other grieving parents' (Domanick 2004: 142).

In addition, victims of crime who fight back in defence of their family or property, such as Tony Martin in Britain, or who wish to avenge themselves against those who have per-petrated terrible crimes against family members – Mark Middleton in New Zealand, for example, threatened to kill the murderer of his stepdaughter if that man's parole appli-cation was successful – can become popular heroes. While their actions can then lead to their own imprisonment as in Martin's case (a five year prison term for manslaughter), or a suspended sentence in Middleton's, that they acted in this way – were 'forced' to act in this way to achieve what they considered to be an appropriate form of justice that the state could not or would not provide – becomes another emblem of the way in which the interests of such 'ordinary people' have been overlooked or dismissed by the criminal justice establishment: ordinary people, whose property the state could not protect; ordinary people, who, in the case of Middleton, had suffered irreparable loss through crime. Not surprisingly, when it seems that the innocent are prosecuted and the guilty are protected, this leads to further distrust of that same establishment.

THE POLITICS OF PENAL POPULISM

Historically, populist movements have been found on both the Left and Right of the political spectrum (Betz 1994). In relation to penal populism, it has thus been argued by Matthews (2005) that this concept can represent both progressive and reactionary forces (and that criminologists writing of such tendencies have largely ignored the former and concentrated on the latter). However, such an assertion misses the point that populist movements are 'of the people but not of the system' (Canovan 1999: 3): *they are outside of the system and are essentially a reaction against the existing political establishment.* Given that the political establishment in the post-war period has (often inaccurately!) come to be associated with a benign liberalism in penal affairs, penal populism will inevitably take a reactionary, regressive stance against this. For this reason, it has been hostile to the rights-based claims usually made by pressure groups campaigning on criminal justice or penal matters. This is because 'rights are tools of an embattled minority while populism sees the majority as embattled and blames excessive deference of the state to rights claims of minorities for that injustice' (Taggart 2000: 116).

In these respects, rather than being of the same order as those minority social movements which, for example, campaign to extend or protect the rights of criminals and curb the excesses of police powers, penal populism attempts to reclaim the penal system for what it sees as the oppressed *majority* and harness it to *their* aspirations rather than those of the establishment, or those of liberal social movements that pull in the opposite direction to which it wants to travel. When rights are referred to in penal populist discourse, it is usually the rights of the public at large to safety and security, and the withdrawal of rights from those very groups (immigrants, asylum seekers, criminals, prisoners) on whose behalf other social movements are campaigning for. In these ways it claims to represent the rights of the general public, not fringe groups or minorities, against what is perceived to be the privileged, highly educated, cosmopolitan elite whose policies have put its security at risk. This also ensures that an inverted egalitarianism emerges out of the resentment that populism can mobilize, one which is 'tinged by the belief that the people are not the equal of their rulers; they are actually better than their rulers' (Taggart 2000: 112). In these respects, Michael Howard proclaimed that:

> The silent majority have become the angry majority . . . in the last thirty years, balance in the criminal justice system has been tilted too far in favour of criminals and against protection of the public. The time has come to put that right. I want to make sure it is criminals that are frightened, not law-abiding members of the public.
>
> (quoted by Zedner 1995: 527)

In this example, it is 'the majority' who are seen as occupying the moral high ground of penal policy debate, not that unnamed group (although the obvious inference is that it is some sector of 'the establishment') who 'in the last thirty years' had been responsible for the imbalance Howard now wished to reverse.

As he went on to indicate, the way to put this right was to develop policy that was more in line with the aspirations of this 'majority'. In so doing, the criminal justice balance would be restored, shifting it away from the interests of criminals and towards those of the law-abiding. Similarly, Ryan (1999: 15, my italics), in the aftermath of New Labour's election victory in 1997, wrote that '[the government] is encouraging communities to believe that they are reclaiming their voice(s) in a crucial area of social regulation, punishment and crime, *something which was taken from them.*' This explains the appeal of much of the sloganizing associated with populist initiatives: 'three strikes', 'truth in sentencing', 'life means life', 'zero tolerance': whatever their strategic effect, these transparent slogans are also emblems of the way in which popular commonsense should order the criminal justice system, rather than the opaque and muddled expertise of the criminal justice establishment.

This sense of anger and resentment over law and order issues provides a staple diet for most of the new populist parties, particularly when they can link these matters with concerns about immigration. For example, 'we try with all our means to have these wild people [i.e. immigrants] which are impossible to integrate, sent home. Home to the conditions they prefer for a society: chaos, murder, robbery and anarchy', claimed a representative of the Danish People's Party (quoted by Rydgren 2004: 20–21). And it has also become ensconced in mainstream politics, providing a point of convergence for both the Left and Right of the political spectrum. This is particularly characteristic of the anglophone world, but also extends well beyond it, including Sweden (Tham 2001) and Spain (Medina-Ariza 2006). While the political right has periodically talked tough on crime since the 1960s (see Beckett 1997), liberal and social democratic politicians have more recently been attracted to the magnetic pull of penal populism, abandoning their more usual position of fighting crime by reducing social inequalities.[5] Bill Clinton was probably the first to do this, leading the Democrats to presidential success in the United States in 1992 and 1996. The traditional North Eastern liberal intelligentsia of the party was kept at bay as he displayed no qualms about the use of the death penalty and was also content to preside over the move to the hyperinflationary prison population for which this country has become infamous (Feely and Simon 1992): out of kilter with his own intelligentsia, certainly, but seemingly in line with public expectations and aspirations. In this way, he provided a template for electoral success which others have since copied (Newburn 2002): Bob Carr, for the Labour Party in the New South Wales state election in 1995 (Hogg and Brown 1998); then New Labour in Britain which formulated its now well known 'tough on crime, tough on the causes of crime' mantra, achieving spectacular election success in 1997 and 2001 (Newburn and Jones 2005); this was replicated by the New Zealand Labour Party in its own successes of 2002 and 2005 (Pratt and Clark 2005). The net result has been that, under these circumstances, political debate about crime and punishment issues can be reduced to a bidding war between the rival main parties, with each bid increasing the intensity and scope of the existing penal system (Newburn 2002). This can then lead to dramatic increases in imprisonment rates, as we see in the examples of two countries where penal populism has been particularly influential: in England the rate increased from 88 per 100,000 of population in 1992 to 145 in 2006; in New Zealand, it increased from 128 in 1995 to 189 in 2006.

A NEW AXIS OF PENAL POWER

In these respects, penal populism has become a phenomenon that represents a dramatic reconfiguration of the power to punish that had been characteristic of post-war modern society. For most of this period, the general public were largely excluded from any involvement in penal affairs. Instead, these matters had been addressed and managed behind the scenes by civil servants working in conjunction with governments and drawing on advice from academic experts and similar elites. In Britain, Loader (2005: 3) characterizes these establishment figures as:

> Platonic guardians ... this closely networked world of colleagues and friends – who moved easily within and between the cloisters of Oxbridge and the departments and dining clubs of Whitehall ... committed to producing and deploying expert knowledge in a bid to handle the crime question in ways that struck a balance between the competing claims of effectiveness and humanity, liberty and order.

As a result, law and order issues were largely residual political matters, marginal to more central governmental concerns such as education, health and welfare. The following extract from a speech made in the Canadian Federal Parliament in a 1975 death penalty debate is a clear illustration of this. The speaker claimed that:

> The cry for law and order has been the cry of nearly every tyrant in history. 'Law and order' was the cry of Hitler when he assassinated nearly one million [sic] Jews. Law and order has always been the cry of people who want to commit violence against others.
>
> (Hansard [195 vol. 1] 830 April 17 1975)

The importance of these comments lies not in their graphic disdain for politicians who exploited concerns about law and order, but in the way in which they represented the predominant thinking about such issues at that time: in democratic societies, law and order should not be politicized and allowed to become a matter of public debate – this was an attribute of totalitarianism.

However, this new axis of penal power revolves much more around the relationship that has been established between governments and those various individuals, groups, and organizations who claim to speak on behalf of 'the people', while the erstwhile guardians 'are left horrified and bemused, lacking a compelling analysis of the ways in which the world has slipped away from them, unsure of how today they can obtain a purchase on it' (Loader 2005: 22). As a result of this shift, concerns about law and order have become much more central to both public and political debate, and expressions of public sentiment can now override scientific expertise and the rationalities of penal bureaucracies. Thus Zimring (1996: 255) wrote, in the aftermath of the California three strikes law, that:

> It may be that the social authority accorded criminal justice experts provided insulation between populist sentiments (always punitive) and criminal justice policies at the legislative, administrative and judicial levels. This insulation prevented the direct domination of policy by anti-offender sentiments that are consistently held by most citizens at most times. What has been changing in recent years is that the insulation that separated public sentiments and criminal justice decisions has been eaten away.

A good illustration of this is provided by the 1999 referendum in New Zealand which received a vote of 91.7 percent in its favour:

> [S]hould there be a reform of our criminal justice system placing greater emphasis on the needs of victims, providing restitution, and compensation for them and imposing minimum sentences and hard labour for all serious violent offences?

Contradictory, incoherent and non-binding, it could have been ignored. Instead, it has since become the central referent of that country's penal policy, and highly influential on the Sentencing Act 2002 (Roberts 2003, Pratt and Clark 2005). The Ministry of Justice (2002: 1) itself acknowledged 'the need to respond to the 1999 referendum which revealed public concern over the sentencing of serious violent offenders. New Zealanders also expressed a desire for better protection from dangerous offenders.' Indeed, when the Sentencing Bill was passed into law, the Justice Minister telephoned the organizer of the referendum to congratulate him on its success. At the same time, precisely because of the closer relationship between populist governments and the general public, policy development can be determined by the need to make immediate responses to exceptional cases as they occur, rather than take a considered approach to more typical offending. Roberts *et al.* (2003: 108) write that:

> Western Australia developed Australia's first mandatory sentencing laws in 1992, aimed specifically at repeat juvenile offenders. The laws were very much developed 'on the run' following a 'rally for justice', partly organized by a talk-back radio host which attracted 20,000 angry protestors to the steps of the legislative assembly complaining about the leniency of the juvenile justice system.

A clear example of the way in which this reconfiguration of penal power has led to very different positionings and ways of addressing crime and punishment can be seen in the New Zealand general elections of 1987 and 2002. Law and order was a major issue in each. In the first, the (centre right) National opposition party tried to ally itself to the police who had initiated the law and order campaign (Pratt and Treacher 1988). Then, this issue had little by way of grass roots public support – the police simply seemed to be using it to generate better conditions of service for themselves, rather than addressing specific crime and punishment issues. At that time, victims of crime, or their relatives, indicated that *they did not wish for any involvement* in these attempts to politicize law and order. Meanwhile, the Labour government tried to *reduce* the issue (cf Garland 1996). It relied on expert opinion to show that increases in criminal statistics were likely to be artefactual rather than real. While it was prepared to acknowledge growing concern about violent crime, it called for a Royal Commission to address the matter – handing the problem over to a tier of experts, rather than allowing itself to be lead by public sentiment. There were no voices at that time claiming to speak on behalf of 'the people'.

In 2002, however, there was now an effective political consensus over law and order as all bar one of the major political parties gave assurances that crime was indeed a real problem and had to be met with more severe sanctions. There was also to be more involvement of the general public in sentencing policy, with regular reference to the support for the 1999 referendum as justification for this. Furthermore, on this occasion, the campaign was not driven by politicians in alliance with the police but by extra-establishment forces: victims' rights and citizens-based lobby groups, the most notable being the Sensible Sentencing Trust (SST), formed in 2001 as a reaction to the conviction of Mark Middleton (see above, p. 19) and apparent government dalliance in implementing the referendum. These groups *led* the campaign, with politicians running to catch up with their demands (the police were now largely silent). Substantial media coverage in the press and on primetime television, a website and two well publicized marches dramatically increased SST's profile in the run-up to the election. The first march took place in Auckland two weeks before it, the second in Wellington a week later. Many of the 900 marchers at the rallies carried handmade wooden crosses, some bearing the names of murder victims.[6] While they were formally intended to be remembrance rallies for the victims of violent crime, amidst SST's claim that the murder rate in New Zealand had increased by 1400 percent over the previous 40 years,[7] they further helped to politicize and publicize law and order, as well as demonstrating this organization's authority and power. *MPs from the main political parties, as well as government ministers*, attended the rallies and addressed the marchers in the penal language of populism, replete with phrases such as 'life should mean life, no parole'; 'there's no reason for parole.'

In these ways, campaigning around law and order involved a public participation that had been entirely absent from the 1987 election. Meanwhile, the criminal justice authorities stood on the sidelines, onlookers as the government, instead of trying to 'define deviance down' seemed ready to talk it up. In such ways, then, penal populism has been able to both set new policy agendas and radically redefine official thinking on crime and punishment.

MORE THAN IMPRISONMENT

These agendas are now reflected in a range of contemporary penal developments. Roberts *et al.* (2003: 50) state that 'the central tool of penal populism is imprisonment.' Certainly, one of its recurring themes has been a demand for longer and harsher sentences of imprisonment. Indeed, in countries where it has been particularly influential – the United States, Britain and New Zealand, for example – it has helped to drive the prison populations of these countries to their highest ever levels. But there is more to penal populism's crime control policy than imprisonment. It also seeks to curtail or abandon altogether many longstanding criminal justice rights which are thought to favour criminals at the expense of law-abiding community members – this was one of the ways to restore the balance that we saw Michael Howard referring to earlier. In England, the Criminal Justice Bill 2002 proposed to strip away defendants' protection from 'double jeopardy'; there was to be limited access to jury trials in the White Paper *Justice for All* (Home Office 2002); the 2002 Mental Health Bill included a proposal for the indefinite detention of individuals with dangerous and severe personality disorders (Tonry 2004a). In the United States, the clawing back of these rights has gone much further. Its sexual predator laws, the first of which was introduced in Washington state in 1989 after a public ballot in its favour, allow for the indefinite civil confinement in a 'special confinement centre' of those so judged (the criteria being a conviction for a sexual offence and an assessment that they have some 'mental abnormality'), after they have served a finite jail sentence for their crime. As Greenlees (1991: 118) has argued, mental abnormality is not a 'psychologically meaningful' condition and virtually anybody could come within this category: and because it is so ill-defined and vacuous, once this adjudication has been made, it then becomes extremely difficult to refute. *Prima facie*, such laws would seem to constitute a flagrant breach of double jeopardy rules. However, because the post-prison confinement is, formally at least, not an additional punishment, the validity of such legislation has been upheld by the Supreme Court: 'the conditions surrounding confinement – essentially the same as conditions for any civilly committed patient – do not suggest a punitive purpose' (Kansas v Hendricks [1997] 521 US 346).

As has the validity of three strikes laws (introduced by public ballot in many states), despite them being in breach of longstanding post-Enlightenment principles relating to the proportionality of punishment to crime (Ewing v California 538 US 11 [2003], 01–6978). As has the validity of laws providing for community notification of sex offenders on release from prison (Connecticut Department of Public Safety v Doe 538 US 11 [2003], 01–1231). As a result of the provisions of the federal Megan's Law in 1996, every state is required to develop some procedures for notifying the public when a sex offender is to be released into their community from prison. This means that these criminals have to carry around with them the shame and humiliation associated with their crimes long after prison – serving time is no longer sufficient to expiate them. Instead of being able to live anonymously on release, they must now face the unremitting awareness that local communities may have of them.[8] President Clinton thus stated when signing the law into effect:

> We respect people's rights but today in America there is no greater right than a parent's right to raise a child in safety and love . . . America warns, if you dare to prey on our children, the law will follow you wherever you go, state to state, town to town.
>
> (Office of the Press Secretary, The White House 25 July 1996)

Again, then, penal populism demands that the rights of victims, the rights of communities, must take precedence over the rights of individual criminals.

Furthermore, penal populism also seeks opportunities to turn the punishment of offenders into a symbolic spectacle of reassurance and vengeance for an onlooking public, humiliation and debasement for its criminal recipients. Thus, the re-introduction of chain gangs to the southern United States in the early 1990s was something more than a

dramatic disavowal of penal reforms that had taken decades
to achieve; in addition, it was an assurance of a return to a
less troublesome, more certain and secure era – the chain
gang had the ability to be a signifier of this:

> I recall seeing chain gangs as a child while driving through the
> states with my parents ... The impression I had was one of
> hard labour and a law-abiding state. That's the image Florida
> needs today – instead of one of innocent citizens and tourists
> being robbed and raped very day.
>
> (Crist 1996: 178)

Similarly, a variety of shaming penalties are now available in
the United States criminal courts. Offenders may be compelled to wear T-shirts that indicate their crimes (Garvey
1998), or display a 'scarlet M' sign in their window to warn
others that they are a convicted sex offender (Bai 1997).
In England, local authorities are encouraged to 'name and
shame' those prosecuted under anti-social behaviour legislation. In Australia, the Northern Territory Punitive Work
Order compelled offenders to wear a black and orange bib
while performing community service:

> Those serving a punitive work order will be clearly obvious to
> the rest of the community. They will be identifiable as punitive
> work offenders either by wearing a special uniform or some
> other label. It is meant to be a punishment that *shames* the
> guilty person.
>
> (Ministerial Statement on the Criminal Justice
> System and Victims of Crime 1996, my italics)

THE SPECIFICITY OF PENAL POPULISM

It must also be emphasized that penal populism is very different from earlier manifestations of populism associated

particularly with the Nixon and Thatcher eras. Certainly, around 1970, Richard Nixon was promoting tough law and order policies – frequently turning on his own establishment ('our judges have gone too far in promoting the doctrine that when a law is broken, society, not the criminal, is to blame,' quoted by Gaubatz 1995: 4) when making his appeals to 'the silent majority' of Americans. In effect, though, he was speaking on their behalf – there was then no mechanism that allowed *them* to speak at this level of governance. However, when he articulated what *he* judged to be their concerns for them, this meant that the public were effectively 'dummy players' with no direct input themselves to penal thinking and policy. Nixon was their ventriloquist. In contrast, penal populism today is built around the idea that the public, or its various representatives, are not mere dummies but can and should have a strong influence on penal affairs. Thus, as Ryan (2003: 135) argues:

> It is not just a matter of governments tapping into moral panics and producing a punitive backlash. Democracy is changing – [the] transmission of public preferences into the heart of government, demanding day by day more attention be given to them is something that all politicians have to learn to live with.

Indeed, as we have seen, governments may be prepared not simply to listen to them but in varying degrees, strike up an alliance with them, or even be led by them.

One of the first indicators of this new kind of partnership came in Mario Cuomo's speech as Mayor of New York state when he posed the question:

> Where does the system go from here . . . it will go where it is sent . . . if we follow the logic that says getting tough on crime means incarcerating all felons, you will see this system grow to around 50,000 inmates . . . *the choice is the people's. You tell us*

*how. You tell us where. The choice has always been the public's
to make.*

(Report of the Department of Correctional Services
1985–86: 18, my italics)

From a level of 30,000 when Cuomo asked the New York
electorate to choose his policy for him, the prison population
of that state had climbed to 71,000 in 1999 – this was the
choice the public had made.

Again, penal populism differs from the authoritarian
populism associated with Thatcherism in Britain. Stuart
Hall (1979: 2) stylized the consequences of this form of
populism as follows:

> By this means – first, forming public opinion, then, disingenu-
> ously, consulting it – the tendency to 'reach for the law' above,
> is complemented by a popular demand to be governed more
> strictly from below. Thereby the drift to law and order above
> secures a degree of popular support and legitimacy amongst
> the powerless, who see no other alternative.

In the New Right discourse Thatcher espoused, the social
democratic trajectory of governance of the post-war period
was blamed for the seemingly ineluctable rise in crime: in
relation to which her authoritarian populism attempted to
impose 'a new regime of social discipline and leadership *from
above* in a society increasingly experienced as rudderless and
out of control' (Hall 1988: 84, my italics). This is exactly the
point: the public had no opinion other than that which was
constructed for them. Also, the solutions to the problems
that this 'manufacture' produced were to be provided by
governments acting on their behalf rather than in conjunction with them. Again, then, *there was no popular movement
outside of the establishment putting forward the view of 'the people'
that politicians could then make some synergy with.* As such, it was

really a form of populism with no substance to it; supposed public voices were expressed almost exclusively through sections of the media rather than through their voluble, loquacious representatives that we find in contemporary popular movements against supposedly liberal sentencing.

Certainly, there had been rhetoric about tougher punishments prior to the Conservative Party's success in the 1979 election, principally about short, sharp shock/army glasshouse style detention centres for young delinquents – as with much of the rhetoric associated with penal populism, a magical solution to a contemporary crime problem, attempting to turn the clock back in this way to some mythical golden crime-free period. After the election victory, however, authoritarian populism led to no great realignment of the penal field. True, there was some curtailment of parole eligibilities and the falling out of favour and demise of post-war elite advisory bodies such as the Advisory Council on the Treatment of Offenders (Ryan 2003). However, the short, sharp shock detention centres were quickly abandoned. Indeed, this episode would seem to constitute a classic example of Bottoms' (1995) notion of populist punitiveness – politicians 'tapping into' the public's punitive stance for their electoral advantage and then jettisoning it – but which is essentially what *'authoritarian'* and not *penal* populism involves. In these respects, the former, because it speaks on behalf of the people, but not 'with' the people, is able to change its policies and programmes as it pleases; speaking for the people in this area ceases to have utility once election success has been assured, once governments have to deal with the complexities of penal problems and the detail of policy. In contrast, the latter phenomenon is much more directly tied into perceived public views about crime and punishment: politicians thus have no monopoly of discourse on these matters and allow themselves to become hostages to whatever fortune this brings.

Overall then, penal populism involves a dramatic recon-figuration of the axis of penal power, with the strategic effect of reversing many of the previous assumptions that had hitherto informed post-war penal policy. There should thus be more prisons rather than fewer; punishment should be turned into a public spectacle rather than take the form of a bureaucratic accomplishment hidden from public view; popular commonsense should be prioritized over the expert knowledge of criminal justice officials. By the same token, because of the much closer linkages between governments and those individuals or organizations who claim to speak on behalf of the public at large, and the much weaker linkages between governments and their own bureaucratic advisers, there is now a much greater likelihood of this collection of ideas being translated into policy.

2

UNDERLYING CAUSES

It might seem a remarkable paradox that penal populism begins to flourish from the early 1990s at exactly the same time as crime levels begin to drop[1] – initially in the United States but then across a range of other Western countries. Bottoms (1995: 47) had specifically linked the rise of populist punitiveness with an increased crime rate: as this is now in decline, then the scope for populism should be shrinking – and yet the opposite has happened. Furthermore, as van Kesteren *et al.* (2000: 83) demonstrate in their survey of 17 industrialized countries, fear of crime has also been falling, in varying degrees, during the late 1990s. Yet at the same time, there has also been 'a general hardening of attitudes towards punishment' (ibid.: 88). How do we explain these apparent contradictions? In this chapter I argue that opportunities for penal populism emerge out of the cumulative and coalescent effect of crucial social changes that have been taking place in modern society from the 1970s. Specifically, the decline of deference has led to a public that is more insistent on having its own 'say' in public affairs; lack of trust in politicians and existing political processes leads to a public that is prepared to support new forms of political expression. Globalization has then accelerated these developments, simultaneously eroding state authority and leaving the public searching for some reassertion of this, to show that someone somewhere, at least, is in control of events.

In these respects, and developing the work of Tyler and Boeckmann (1997), penal populism emerges out of concerns to restore a disintegrating social and moral cohesion that these changes have brought about rather than as a specific response to crime problems. This does not mean, however, that there is *no* relationship between crime levels and penal populism. Indeed, rising crime up to at least the early 1990s can be seen as one indicator,[2] amongst numerous others, of this disintegrating social and moral cohesion: in addition, perceptions that crime is *still* rising continue and add to the sense of decline and disintegration that populism claims it is able to address.

THE DECLINE OF DEFERENCE

Let us begin by returning to the 1999 New Zealand referendum. Until this was so decisively approved by the electorate there had been little opposition of any note to it save, ironically, from women against violence groups (Pratt and Clark 2005). Liberal elites in that country had disdainfully ignored it: how could such a proposal, so plainly incoherent and illogical, be taken seriously by government? Nonetheless, after the vote, it became apparent that it was to be taken very seriously indeed by government. At this point the Secretary of Justice expressed his scepticism about its value to Parliament's Justice and Electoral Select Committee. The question was confusing and it was difficult to tell exactly what the electorate had been voting for. He was reported as saying 'we all witnessed people in polling booths scratching their heads and thinking "what does this mean?" ' (*The*

Dominion 17 February 2000: 1).[3] However, the Christchurch shopkeeper who organized the referendum was not deflated or silenced by such patrician dismissal. In media interviews he expressed his outrage at the 'sneaky backdoor tactics of politicians and their officials' to discredit it, and attacked the civil servant's implicit elitism:

> [A]re they [sic] saying the public is thick? . . . you can't twist the result around and start shanghai-ing it. I'm a facts and figures merchant and what we have before us is a document that has gone through the whole process . . . As far as I'm concerned, the question was plain English.
>
> (ibid.)

It confirmed his view that the only opposition to it had been from elite, unrepresentative groups such as 'upper class individuals and a few trendies.'[4]

The nature of his response to a senior civil servant – indeed that he could hold the national media in his thrall as he made it – points to one of the reasons for the rise of penal populism. This is known as 'the decline of deference' (Nevitte 1996), a phenomenon taking place across much of modern society which involves a rejection by a large section of the general public of the hitherto unquestioned acceptance of authority or establishment figures and the values they represent. A prominent and celebrated theme in political discourse today,[5] its decline ensures that those establishment figures who had previously had unchallenged and unquestioned power by virtue of the fact that they *were* part of the establishment now find that this is no longer the case. In these respects, up to the 1970s, it was not simply that the general public were actively excluded from any legitimate participation in penal affairs; in addition, it was generally assumed by members of the establishment that, far from wanting to have any influence at all on such matters, they would happily leave them to 'their betters' – those in high office in the government and civil service. After all, as Professor of Politics Richard Rose put the matter in 1965:

> *Because there is trust in the good intentions of governors*, it is possible for public figures to make public policy in considerable privacy. This privacy is strengthened by strong legal sanctions against those revealing unpublished government documents, and by strong cultural sanctions upholding the privacy of governmental deliberations.
>
> (quoted by Ryan 2003: 37, my italics)

Today, such a statement seems extraordinarily anachronistic. At the time it was made, though, an enormous social distance separated establishment figures from 'ordinary people'. It was not simply the legal and cultural codes of protection enshrining their work that placed them beyond scrutiny and examination; in addition – certainly in Britain which seemed to be the exemplar of a deferential society (Almond and Verba 1963) – there was a built-in class deference from the rest of society to such elites. Unlike most other people at that time, those employed in the professions of the elite would almost certainly have been educated at private schools and the most prestigious universities, thereafter enjoying the patronage that being part of the establishment brought with it. They were assumed to constitute the 'natural' class of government on the basis of their lineage, education and wealth, which the structure of British society then perpetuated. Sampson (1962: 154) thus wrote that:

> [J]udges have always come from a small and conservative section of the community . . . Of the forty two judges who list their education in Who's Who, seven came from Christ Church, Oxford, six from Trinity, Cambridge, and only one from a

redbrick university. Winchester produced five, Rugby four, Eton three: eleven came from grammar schools.

Similarly, of the Civil Service Secretaries and Deputy Secretaries in 1950:

> Over four-fifths were stated in their Who's Who biographies to be members of one or more London clubs; and of these club members, 70 percent belonged to one or other of five which were, in order of popularity, the Oxford and Cambridge, the Union, the United University, the Reform and the Athenaeum.
>
> (Kelsall 1955: 182)

In such ways, then, the exclusivity of these elites was both guaranteed and perpetuated.

From the 1970s, however, there has been a decline in the assumption that such groups have some natural right to govern. Broad sections of the public have regularly demanded the right to be involved in matters of governance themselves, have sought the right to determine for themselves how public policy should be developed. They are no longer satisfied with this being decided on their behalf 'behind the scenes'. As Hough (2003: 149) has put the matter:

> Growing public expectations of public services need to be understood in the context of declining deference. A deferential public would expect public institutions to define for them what services they needed and expected. A less deferential public would do this job themselves.

As, indeed, the wide-ranging single issue pressure groups that form around a variety of social issues including law and order regularly insist on the right to do so.

As such, the cultural reticence and deference that used

to lead to a general acquiescence with the existing power structure of modern society has been dissolving. There is no longer the assumption and expectation that governance and policy issues should be determined by elites and then digested unquestioningly as a matter of course by the rest of the population. Nevitte (1996: 39) argues that such developments are the natural consequence of the way in which post-war social reforms raised the living standards and aspirations of the whole population in previously deferential societies such as Britain: 'one of the significant structural changes accompanying the shift to advanced industrialism is the emergence of a more highly educated public.' Those in government or other establishment sectors would no longer be viewed as the social superiors of the rest of society – many of whom would now be able to compete with them in terms of educational achievement. Thus in the United Kingdom, the number of tertiary students has increased from less than 500,000 in 1960 to 2.4 million in 2002 (with corresponding increases in similar societies).[6] By 1980, these changes were already having an impact on the appointment of civil service Permanent Secretaries: 'in 1950 one third had been to a leading public school . . . it is now one in eight' (Kellner and Crowther-Hunt 1980: 193).

In these respects, the decline of deference can have a two-fold impact on the rise of penal populism. First, with developments in Britain as an exemplar, it can transform the relationship between the government and its civil service, fundamentally weakening the ability of the criminal justice authorities to keep penal policy securely within its own grasp, thereby leaving it open to populist influences. Second, with developments in the United States as an exemplar, it can weaken the authority of criminal justice officials – sentencers and parole board administrators – thereby opening up the judicial process to more political and public influences and expectations.

Weakening the civil service

As a harbinger of such developments, Inglehart (1977: 8) noted a 'growing divergence of outlook between new elites oriented towards scientific and professional goals and other older elites attached to their own particular firms or bureaucracies.' What has happened since then is that the latter, exemplified by the civil service, have increasingly been seen as a barrier standing in the way of the aspirations of the former – the risk-takers and wealth creators as they have come to be known. This change in values brought about a profound influence on the government's relations with the civil service which up to the 1970s had enjoyed deferential privileges and authority. However, in 1979, Margaret Thatcher's election success enshrined political debate within the hegemony of neo-liberal polity. Now, the civil service as a bastion of privilege and protection was seen as a major obstacle – part of an inflated public service/state industries sector with overmighty trade unions to match – to the creation of the more dynamic, meritocratic 'enterprise society' (Hennessey 1989: 632) that Thatcher had in mind. It exemplified wasteful, unproductive public expenditure: it offered secure employment with a generous state-funded pension on retirement at a time when job security was ceasing to exist for many others in the workforce.

It also embodied class distinction, with no open competition for appointments, thereby allowing the power and privilege of the establishment to entrench and perpetuate itself. Kellner and Crowther-Hunt (1980: 138) thus wrote that 'a new Permanent Secretary is typically a 53-year-old Oxbridge graduate with about 30 years in the civil service.' It had favoured the appointment of the 'amateur all rounder', in the words of the Fulton Committee (1968: 9), while 'scientists, engineers and members of other specialist classes are frequently given neither the full responsibilities and opportunities nor the corresponding authority they ought to have.' Since then, however, the British civil service has been dramatically restructured (Mountfield 2000), with a view to making it more transparent, publicly accountable and fiscally responsible. The service was subject to a range of cost-cutting exercises and efficiency probes, with a view to developing a management culture based on merit. Its size has been considerably reduced, with numbers declining from 746,000 in 1978 to 480,000 in 2003 (Wilson 2003: 38). Overall, the emphasis was to be on the achievement of targets set by government, and service and accountability, in line with the Citizens Charter of 1991, rather than the obfuscation, superiority and disdain it had come to be associated with before. Civil servants were required to publish annual targets and report on performance. To ensure that management would be more in line with government thinking, chief executives from outside the civil service were increasingly appointed on fixed-term contracts, allowing their removal if the prescribed targets were not achieved. Not only this, but numbers of 'special advisers' (or 'commissars') to Ministers were appointed on a purely political basis, with a view to ensuring that in these senior ranks the civil service lost its neutrality and would more readily act in line with government aspirations rather than, at best, as mediators of them; at worst, as impenetrable barriers to them.

At the beginning of this process, the Home Office was shielded, to a degree, from such developments (Lewis 1997). Insular and hierarchical, it was described in the early 1990s as 'the last great unreformed Whitehall department' (see Ryan 2003: 103). In the 1980s, its liberal stance on penal affairs had survived – even flourished – as a result of the assiduous *informal* contacts Permanent Secretary David Faulkner had pursued with sympathetic elites outside of government (Windlesham 1998, Ryan 2003), even if formal contacts had by then been brought abruptly to a halt. Thereafter, however, internal restructuring and the competing influence of outside pressure groups and think tanks (Downes and Morgan 1997, Wacquant 2004) has had the effect of undermining its grip on policy development, making it vulnerable to populist influences; as has the succession, from the early 1990s, of Home Secretaries who have shown a tolerance for levels of imprisonment that are anathema to the patrician principles of 'decency' that used to inform policy development (Loader 2005). Now, rather than being provided with the opportunity to lead penal thinking, the civil service may find itself cut off and marooned from it. Lewis (1997: 116) thus writes that, by the mid 1990s:

> The Prison Service found itself moving in the opposite direction to a hardening public opinion. It took no more than a few well-publicized disasters – temporarily released prisoners committing further crimes, in some cases violent – to create political pressure for a U-turn.

As Lewis intimates, the Civil Service was no longer able to restrict the flow of information, no longer strong enough to ride waves of public dissent when they surfaced, but instead was increasingly compelled to follow in the wake of such extra-establishment influences.

Overall, the result has been a more compliant service, less obstructive than would almost certainly have previously been the case to the more punitive legislation that Conservative and Labour governments, inspired by populist concerns and issues, have pushed through since the early 1990s. Indeed, it has become part of:

> [A] political culture dominated by actors preoccupied with being seen to react immediately and resolutely to mass-mediated, emotionally charged and urgently pressed public concerns

about crime and disorder ... while at the same time feeling they can proceed without the 'culture of deliberation' that was once the hallmark of how crime and penal matters were weighed and responded to by government.

(Loader 2005: 21)

The extent of the change, and indicative of an almost reverse relationship of deference between the civil service and the general public that has since been cultivated, is evident in the remarkable statement contained in the Home Office (2002: 86) White Paper, *Justice for All*: 'the people are sick and tired of a sentencing system that does not make sense.' In the days of deference, of course, 'the system' ostensibly did make sense to those mandarins who maintained control of its policy direction; whether it made sense to anyone else was largely irrelevant to them. Now, though, the service is more amenable to government demands and thereby less able to resist the populist influences that inform these:

Home Office policy making no longer follows once standard processes of informal consultation ... portions of criminal justice policy making have become somewhat less cohesive, coherent, controlled and centralized as they come under the sway of devolution, 'contracting out', and external consultants ... *The newest modes of policy making are themselves the fruits of a new politics of populism, moralism and the market.*

(Rock 1995: 2, my italics)

In effect, wealth, privilege and political power have become democratized – these are no longer the exclusive possession of those with blue blood and an honourable lineage. The 'Platonic guardians' who had previously presided over penal affairs can now expect challenge and confrontation rather than acquiescence: the opinion of the shopkeeper petition organizer can be at least as good as that of the senior civil servant. In the past, there may well have been law and order groups campaigning for harsher sentences from beyond the establishment, but they would then have received little support, if any, from those inside it. Public involvement in penal affairs was looked upon with disdain, as is evident in Louis Blom Cooper's address to the Howard League in 1977, itself, to use Ryan's (1978) phrase, 'an acceptable pressure group': 'there are dangers in a pressure group in the penal field of broadening its appeal to the public in general' (quoted by Ryan 2003: 37). Now, however, the exclusive ownership of penal debate that such groups previously possessed has been opened up to much more regular and obvious public and political influences.

Diminishing the authority of criminal justice officials

In the United States in particular, the authority and stature of criminal justice officials has also been undermined by the decline of deference. Here, though, this seems to have been brought about not so much by the fragmentation of social class that has taken place in Britain but instead by the way in which the collapse of the rehabilitative ideal undercut their expertise (Martinson 1974, Allen 1981). This probably had a greater impact on the United States than most other anglophone countries because the concept of treatment and rehabilitation had become so much more deeply embedded in its penal system, with considerably more investment in the specialist knowledge of experts advising on such matters (see, for example, Dession 1937).[7] As a result, up to the mid 1970s, treatment and rehabilitation had been the firm cornerstone of post-war penal policy in that country, signifying not simply the authority of the experts who administered these strategies but, in addition, a commitment to a humane, rational, scientific approach to crime control. Thereafter, however, this penal trajectory, based largely around judicial discretion and parole board adjudication procedures, was extensively criticized from both the Right and Left of the political spectrum: treatment/rehabilitation was regarded as ineffectual and an expensive waste of taxpayer's money from the Right; but the projects it led to – particularly the use of the indeterminate prison sentence allowing for the detention of its recipients until their criminogenic 'illnesses' were 'cured' – were seen as violating human rights and sanctioning illegitimate expressions of state power and control by the Left.

In essence, the concept of rehabilitation had become a failure and a fraud, its critics maintained. They favoured instead what has become known as the 'justice model' or 'just deserts theory' (see Fogel 1975, von Hirsch 1976) as the central philosophy of punishment. This new thinking was built around rights-based rather than welfare-based criminal justice policy; in particular, the right to be treated as a rational, responsible citizen rather than one who was deficient and dependent. It thereby necessitated the replacement of open-ended indeterminate sentencing with finite, determinate sentencing. This should also be mandatory, to curtail both judicial and parole board discretion and autonomy. Thus the origins of the United States sentencing commissions – introduced to devise sentencing norms and values and often implemented in elaborate grids where the only room for judicial manoeuvre is to fix the particular case at a precise point in this – began on the basis that 'the previously unfettered discretion accorded federal trial judges needed to be structured' (United States Sentencing Commission 2005: 2).

Since then some of them (as with sentencing councils that have been established elsewhere in the anglophone world) have become increasingly democratized. They may thus include citizens' representatives and victim advocates as well as judges, lawyers and elected officials, with some specifically requiring that the guidelines for sentencing that are developed be consistent with 'the views of the public' (Freiberg 2003); others maintain an awkward balance between the competing factions that such commissions can contain: that for Alabama seeks to 'maintain judicial discretion to permit individualised sentencing as warranted', but also 'promotes truth in sentencing'; it is designed to 'prevent prison overcrowding' and also prevent 'the premature release of inmates'.[8]

Essentially, though, the advent of 'just deserts' signalled an end not just to rehabilitation but also to the 'romantic tolerance extended to deviants in society' (Hudson 1987: 59), which there had always been a space for when the sentence had to fit the criminal not the crime (Zimring and Johnson 2006). In addition, rehabilitation had also been able to provide a barrier to political debate about sentencing: the concept was 'owned' by 'human sciences' experts whose pedagogy and discourse then occluded the whole subject (Davies 1985). 'Just deserts', in contrast, insists on proportionality and determinacy. The sentence has to fit the offence, not the offender. However, what constitutes a proportionate punishment is always going to be a value judgement, which as a result of the sentencing reforms that have been introduced in the United States especially, will no longer be an exclusive reflection of judicial values. Furthermore, as the authority of the criminal justice officials has been undermined, that of victims and their representatives has been considerably enhanced, and, certainly in the United States (Strang 2002), they can bring particularly punitive values to the punishment process. They demand their own legitimate place in sentencing and parole board adjudications, with victim impact statements (a procedure which has now spread to numerous other jurisdictions) shifting the balance of such decision-making away from supposedly objective, social scientific diagnosis of the offender and their difficulties to a much more emotive and volatile consideration of the harm they have inflicted on others, providing the opportunity for a more vindictive rather than rehabilitative approach to punishment.

In such ways, the restriction of judicial discretion in sentencing and parole boards in early release decision-making has steadily become a normalized feature of the United States penal system. Without the barrier of deference that used to be placed in front of political and populist influences from outside of the criminal justice establishment, common sense concepts such as 'three strikes' and 'truth in sentencing' have been allowed to become normative values of the sentencing system. These concepts exemplify the way in which judicial discretion has given way to mandatory sentencing, determined by publicly elected officials or citizens' ballots; and the way in which time served in prison may be determined at sentencing and made known to the general public rather than covered over by the opaque processes of non-elected parole boards. As Zimring and Johnson (2006: 17) write, 'as soon as the chain of expertise is discredited, the man in the street (or his state representative) is every bit the expert as the judge, the parole board, or the correctional administrator.'

THE DECLINE OF TRUST IN POLITICIANS AND POLITICAL PROCESSES

However, this new involvement of ordinary people or those who claim to speak on their behalf in public and penal affairs is also a reflection of a concomitant decline in trust in politicians and the political processes that have brought them to power: when there is no trust in such individuals or institutions to act on behalf of 'the people', then the people will begin to claim this right for themselves, albeit through different channels. Some 40 years ago, Almond and Verba (1963: 490) wrote that:

> The role of social trust and cooperativeness as a component of civic culture cannot be overemphasised ... social trust facilitates political cooperation among the citizens and without it democratic politics is impossible. It probably also enters into a citizen's relation with political elites ... the maintenance of elite power [is] essential in a democracy ... the sense of trust in the political elite – the belief that they are not alien and extractive forces, but part of the same political community – makes citizens willing to turn power over to them.

Such statements again seem remarkably anachronistic in the light of a MORI opinion poll in Britain which found that 'while trust in individual professions has generally remained static, trust in institutions has declined, in some cases quite significantly' (Duffy 2003). Indeed, trust in the institutions of government, parliament, the legal system and the press in Britain is well below the European norm (European Commission 2004). No doubt as a result, while in 1974 in response to the question 'how much do you trust the British government of any party to place the needs of the nation before the interests of their own political party?', 40 percent said always/mostly and 57 percent some/never; in 1999 the figures were 21 percent and 75 percent respectively (Duffy 2003). Furthermore, between 1999 and 2004 politicians and government received least support to the question 'how satisfied are you with the way the following types of people do their jobs?' In polls between 1983 and 2003, politicians (with journalists) were thought each time to be least likely to be telling the truth (Worcester 2003). Similarly, United States Gallup polls indicate that lack of trust in government reached its nadir in 1994 at 74 percent. In 2001 this received a temporary boost after 9/11 and in October that year had dropped to 38 percent; however, in 2005 it was back to 65 percent (Gallup Organization 2005). Changes in voting patterns for general or presidential elections would seem to be further evidence of this decline. In Britain this fell from a 78 percent turnout in 1992 to 59 percent in 2001 (with a slight rise to 61 percent in 2005). Recent additions to the democratic process such as election to the European Parliament have seen even smaller turnouts (see Furedi 2004: 33). In the United States, 61.9 percent of the voting age population cast a vote in the 1964 presidential election; in 2000 this had declined to 51.2 percent (United States Census Bureau 2004–5: 257).

There were similar findings in Canada in a Citizens' Forum on Canada's Future (1991: 1): '[people] do not feel that their governments, especially at the federal level, reflect the will of the people, and they do not feel that citizens have the means at the moment to correct this.' Further studies indicate that:

> Canadians believe that 'MPs are not responsive to the needs of constituents' . . . three out of four Canadians agree with the statement, 'I don't think that the government cares much what people like me think', up from 1 in 2 in 1965.
>
> (Nevitte 1996: 26)

Similarly, Cross (2000: 4) found that 'there is substantial evidence that Canadians are decidedly dissatisfied with their present political arrangements and institutions.' In New Zealand, a Mood of the Nation Report (UMR Research Limited, 2004) found that politicians enjoyed the least respect of the seventeen occupations assessed by those surveyed. Voter registration had declined to 77 percent in 2002, its lowest level in the post-war period. Indeed, the main reason for the change from its first past the post electoral system to proportional representation and referenda in the mid 1990s was because of this disenchantment and collapse of government authority. An opinion poll in 1990 indicated that, of the two main political parties, only

11 percent of the electorate thought that the Labour Party was trustworthy, and only 19 percent National. In contrast, there was an 84 percent vote in favour of electoral change in the 1993 election (Pratt and Clark 2005). Such trends in these particular societies have been replicated at a more general level in the survey of the World Economic Forum (2003: 1):

> [A] just completed global opinion poll reveals that trust is not only declining in institutions across the world, but leaders themselves have suffered declining public trust over the past year and today enjoy less trust than the institutions they lead.

What is it that lies behind these levels of distrust and dissatisfaction? It might be thought that this can be attributed to the incompetence or duplicity of individual politicians: Richard Nixon and Watergate, for example; the corruption that came to be associated with the ruling Conservative Party in Britain in the 1990s; the deceit that has come to be associated with George Bush Jnr and Tony Blair over the war in Iraq. This does not explain why it is, though, that this distrust has also become so manifest in a country such as New Zealand which is recognized as one of the least politically corrupt countries in the world (Transparency International 2005). As such, I want to suggest that the reason for it is not to be found in the venality of individual politicians (although this does nothing to improve levels of trust) but, instead, in the perceived inability of the existing political processes to look after and respond to the needs of 'ordinary people' – that key constituency from which populism draws its support.

In Britain and New Zealand this begins around the mid 1970s with expressions of dissatisfaction with the post-war welfare state. By this time, despite the massive investment and political commitment to this:

[W]elfare problems did not get 'solved': instead they became an object of policy and administration and, in the process, became more visible, more complex and more demanding of state funds. Even where welfare solutions were effective – for example in combating destitution or malnutrition, or poor health and housing – this still tended to produce more rather than fewer cases.

(Garland 2001: 93)

Furthermore, the welfare structure that had been developed in these and similar societies[9] by this juncture seemed only to reward the feckless and the irresponsible while obstructing and restricting the route to success of the meritorious and the worthy through high levels of taxation. In Britain, the failure of the post-war welfare state was exemplified in the late 1970s by the sense of social and economic disintegration that then seemed to be taking place (as reflected in strikes, growing unemployment, inflation, intervention by the IMF), and the powerlessness of the Labour government to stem the tide. In New Zealand, the repressive levels of bureaucratic governance that had been developed made that country in the early 1980's seem to have more in common with the regulatory nature of Eastern bloc societies rather than the Western democracies (Pratt and Clark 2005).

As such, the apparent bankruptcy of welfarism allowed for the ascendancy of the neo-liberal polity espoused by Mrs Thatcher in Britain from 1979 and Ronald Reagan in the United States from 1980. It was put into effect in New Zealand in 1984 by an incoming Labour Government and thereafter, *but in varying degrees*, found a place in most other Western countries. Hostile to welfarism, designed to set individuals free from 'big government', in neo-liberalism's most intense form, the ineffective and morally corrosive welfare policies propagated by establishment elites would be cut back and individual citizens would be given greater freedom of choice over the course they wanted their lives to run. Penalizing levels of direct taxation would thus be replaced with less intrusive indirect taxes. However, the euphoria which has usually followed such dramatic changes has also tended to evaporate very quickly. A much greater reluctance to intervene to secure collapsing businesses by governments, deregulation and privatization – all of them necessary strategies to bring about increases in material wealth and transform the economic structure of modern society – have also led to the collapse of employment security, now accompanied by an ever more flimsy welfare safety net in support. As a result, from the early 1980s, most of those societies which have incorporated some elements of neo-liberal policies have known periods of dramatically high unemployment, as well as high interest rates and high inflation. Even if, in the last few years, this pattern has lessened in most of these societies – indeed unemployment has been at near record lows in some with acute labour shortages – the onset of part-time or sessional or casual temporary work (only to be interspersed with further periods of unemployment) has become the norm for many, with few employment benefits or rights.

Certainly, the reorganization of the labour force may have led to greater increases in personal wealth for many, but it has also led to new vulnerabilities and risks, from which there will be little if any state assistance. In Britain, the democratization of wealth and privilege and the unforeseen risks this carries with it is exemplified by the increased recruitment in the 1980s of Lloyd's 'names' – that is, those who would underwrite insurance risks in return for what in most years was a healthy dividend (around £29,000 per annum from the 1960s to the late 1980s [Raphael 1994]) – from the middle classes, giving them an entry to what had previously been upper class territory. Unfortunately, most of these new 'names' had ignored or were unaware of the *unlimited* liability that came with these agreements and which they then had to meet, often precipitating their own ruin, after a series of massive insurance claims around 1990. The same processes that can lead to riches probably undreamt of by most people in the 1970s have at the same time the power to bring about their destruction. In such ways, in addition to whatever material advantages it has produced for individual citizens, the shift from welfarism to neo-liberalism has also engineered a much more *precarious* society, compounded by the sense that 'the established political class is no longer able to resolve the most basic problems, [and] that politicians generally are too absorbed with themselves to be able to adapt to a rapidly changing world' (Betz 1994: 41).

GLOBALIZATION

This sense of precariousness has then been accelerated by the impact of globalization – the spread of information, people and products around the world, along with international commerce which free market ideology and practice allows (Baker and Roberts 2005). At the same time, globalization is also associated with harmonization: that is to say, the need for a society's cultural, social and economic and even penal policies to be brought into line with those of supra-national organizations, such as the EU. A given society's policies may thus no longer seem to be of its own making but instead may be determined by non-elected, non-accountable organizations meeting at distant points on the globe, or sometimes only meeting in cyber space. Little wonder, then, that the most popular answer to the question 'who runs Britain' in a BBC poll broadcast on 28 January 2006[10] was 'the EU Commissioner' (followed by press baron Rupert Murdoch). The oil price rises of the 1970s were perhaps the first indication of the vulnerability of individual governments to supra-national business organizations and conglomerates – on this occasion the OPEC cartel. Since then, along with the spreading tentacles of multi-national corporations, there have been regular occasions when national sovereignty seems to have been at the mercy of organizations such as the UN, the EU, the World Trade Organization, the Group of Five, the Group of Seven and the Group of Eight, the World Court, the International Criminal Court, the UN Commission on Human Rights or the EU Commission on Human Rights, the International Atomic Energy Agency, NATO, the ASEAN Regional Forum, the General Agreement on Tariffs and Trade – and so we could continue. Indeed, international non-government organizations grew from virtually zero to nearly 5,500 during the course of the twentieth century (see Held *et al*. 1999).

Similarly, the spread of new information technology allows for the rise of a new world financial order beyond the control of individual governments. As Giddens (2002: 9) writes:

> [I]n the new global electronic economy, fund managers, banks, corporations as well as millions of individual investors, can transfer vast amounts of capital from one side of the globe to another at the click of a mouse. As they do so they can destabilise what might have seemed rock solid economies.

On such occasions, individual states can seem powerless to act, powerless before the might of such supra-state forces. For example, in Britain, the Conservative Government in 1992, on what became known as 'Black Wednesday' after massive spending in international currency markets to fend off speculators, was forced to withdraw the pound from the European Exchange Rate Mechanism.[11] Ultimately, the international speculators who profited from this to an estimated cost to the British taxpayer of £3.3 billion were able to defeat the intentions of the British government. From that point on, support for and trust in the Conservative Party collapsed.

Under these circumstances, it can indeed seem, as Bauman (1997: 58) has argued, that no-one is in control of the nation's destiny:

> The deepest meaning conveyed by the idea of globalisation is that of the indeterminate, unruly and self-propelled character of world affairs, the absence of a centre, of a controlling clerk, of a board of directors, of a managerial office . . . with the effect that we are thrown into a vast open sea with no navigation charts and all the marker buoys sunk and barely visible, we have only two choices left: we may rejoice in the breath-taking view of new discoveries – or we may tremble out of fear of drowning.

Although in reality, most of us are probably likely to experience both of these sensations: celebrating the new routes we can explore towards self-enhancement and personal fulfilment that globalization and economic deregulation have made possible on the one hand; but, on the other, fearing what will happen if we stumble along the way during the course of these explorations, as the result of the new and imponderable dangers that may be lying in wait for us.

And it is precisely for these reasons – at the exact time that the government no longer seems to be in charge of events – that we find a greater citizen involvement in politics itself, albeit alternative forms of politics and forms of political expression which eschew existing outlets because these have become so tainted with disillusionment. Inglehart (1999: 294) thus refers to the paradox of a 'declining respect for authority amongst the publics of advanced industrial society' – but which at the same time:

> [G]ives rise to growing support for democracy. This phenomenon has contributed to declining trust in the United States

and other advanced industrial societies ... although hierarchical political parties are losing control over their electorates, and elite-directed forms of participation such as voting are stagnant or declining, elite challenging forms of participation are becoming more widespread.

As we have seen, this includes demands for more active political representation and consultation in the form of a new politics, which in many ways bypasses the previous routes through which political issues had been played out. Instead of placing trust in mainstream political parties and the traditional class-based loyalties that made up their platform of support in the past, there are flirtations with those politicians and parties who speak to populist concerns: they offer simple, commonsense solutions to problems the established political and democratic processes seem unable to resolve. At the same time, as individuals have become more mobile as well as more educated, less tied not only to their own communities but to their own position in society, hierarchical class distinctions and rigidities break down, further weakening political loyalties and acquiescence based around class (Giddens 2001). Overall, the product is a more volatile and distrustful electorate, one that is more readily prepared to support 'outsider' politics and politicians against established 'insiders'.

CRIME, INSECURITY AND SOCIAL CHANGE

In conjunction with this disenchantment for long established bastions of Western democratic society, many of the familiar landmarks in private life which provided security and stability no longer do so. For much of modern society, one of the ways in which individuals had been able to guard themselves against 'existential anxiety' was by developing:

[A] framework of ontological security of some sort, based on routines of various forms. People handle dangers and the fears associated with them in terms of the emotional and behavioural 'formulae' which have come to be part of their everyday behaviour and thought.

(Giddens 1991: 44)

However, it is clear that many of the conditions necessary for such formulae are no longer in place, or that the formulae have been rewritten to such an extent that the answers they provide are no longer understandable or applicable. While the decline of certainty and security in the workplace is one example of this, the shattering of family life and all that was expected of it is another. In 1970 in England, there were around eight marriages for every divorce (415,487 to 57,421); by 1999, the ratio was closer to three to two (304,800 to 171,310); a similar pattern prevails for Canada, Australia and New Zealand (United Nations 1971–2000). In the United States (perhaps because of more liberal divorce laws already in existence), the ratio was already three to one at the start of this period, but had come down to two to one by 1999 (ibid.). In addition, marriage itself has been in sharp decline as a social practice, giving way to more transient cohabiting practices: less fraught, if or when break up takes place, but by the same token, lending themselves to further impermanence and a continuous shifting of responsibilities and obligations, bringing more uncertainties and insecurities, more journeys into the unknown rather than stability and security.

Similarly, we find a decline in the authority of religion and massive drops in church attendance. For example, in Britain:

The Catholic Church . . . has seen its attendances drop markedly and at an accelerating pace. In the 1980s attendances fell by 14 percent. In the 1990s they fell by 28 percent. The second largest, the Church of England, saw attendances fall from 1,671,000 in 1979 to 980,000 in 1999 – a fall of 24 percent for the 1980s and 23 percent for the 1990s. The United Reformed Church suffered a similar fate. Only the very small Orthodox Church grew ... Overall, attendance for these four churches fell over two decades from 3.9 million to 2.4 million.

(Bruce 2000: 64)

In the United States, the number of non-evangelical Protestants declined from 46.2 percent to 34.2 percent of professing Christians in the same period (Barrett *et al.* 2001). That there has only been growth in fundamentalist expressions of Christianity in this period is itself an indication of the need to cling to something that has a clear, unequivocal identity and will provide security when the established order seems to be collapsing all around.

Fukuyama (1995) provides further illustrations of this fraying of important pillars of social cohesion, such as declining involvement in parent teacher associations and trade union membership. Again, the growth in civil litigation in the United States especially over the same period (LaFree 1998) is a reflection of the way in which inter-personal bonds have fragmented: lack of trust in other individuals necessitates a greater reliance on formal rather than informal procedures to resolve everyday disputes. In addition, it may also reflect the way in which weak inter-personal bonds allow an unforgiving vindictiveness to replace more tolerant forbearance that might otherwise regulate the conduct of such relations. Overall, then, many of the necessary ingredients for transmitting a civic culture and thereby binding the individual to society at large have been eroded. The ontological security that these and other foundation blocks of modern society had once been able to provide has been replaced instead by ontological *insecurity*. These new areas of experience that have replaced them then require constant negotiation and awareness of the perils they might contain.

Meanwhile, the ever accelerating crime rate that ran through virtually all Western countries from the 1960s to the early 1990s made such tasks increasingly fraught and perilous. For example, LaFree (2002: 890) shows that in the United States 'from 1960 to 1975, homicide rates nearly doubled and robbery rates nearly quadrupled.' There were even more dramatic increases in violent crime in California, which he goes on to argue is the source for the particularly punitive legislation that subsequently emerged in that state. Certainly, as crime continued to grow in the late twentieth century, the public increasingly demanded that the government legislate for harsher penalties to provide protection for themselves and to incapacitate criminals. When governments seemed slow to act, or when the criminal justice authorities seemed to work to different principles, then a major lacunae opened up between such establishment forces and an increasingly anxious and insecure general public – increasing the disenchantment with the state and its authorities and generating support for politicians and populist organizations who placed themselves on the public's side of this division. Savelsberg (1994: 929) demonstrates that, from the 1960s to the 1990s, the proportion of Americans believing that courts were not dealing harshly enough with criminals increased from 48 percent in 1965 to 66 percent in 1972 to 85 percent in 1978: thereafter it continued to stay at this level for the next 20 years. The same pattern is found in similar societies, if at somewhat lower levels. Roberts *et al.* (2003: 29), on Canada, show that opinion ranged from between 61 percent and 69 percent between 1990 and 1999, that courts were too lenient and not punitive enough. In the United Kingdom, it ranged between 71 percent and 74 percent between 1987 and 2001 (ibid.). Not only that, but fear of crime, not a significant issue in most Western countries in the immediate post-war years (Zimring and Johnson 2006) had become endemic in most of them by the 1990s (see, for example, Robinson *et al*. 1990, Scheingold 1991, van Dijk and Mayhew 1993, Mayhew *et al*. 1994, Roberts and Stalans 1997, Mirrlees-Black *et al*. 1998)-

Indeed, the unrelenting growth of crime from the 1960s to the early 1990s had become one of the most obvious hallmarks of a society where so many of the previous indicators of security and stability seemed to be breaking down, one of the most obvious hallmarks of a society where authority – of the state, the law, elites, individual citizens – seemed to be increasingly disregarded and where governments, irrespective of political colour, no longer seemed to have any control over such events and seemed powerless to stop the disintegration taking place.

In one of the first official responses to the rising crime rate that then set the standard for the rest of the welfare era, President Johnson appointed the National Crime Commission in 1965. It was made up of 'men and women of distinction': of the 19 members, 15 were attorneys with one newspaper publisher and three academics, all of whom were law professors. In other words, the way to respond to popular fears about crime problems was to entrust the matter to a group of elitist experts and look to them to provide solutions to it. In fact, the Commission came to predictable conclusions:

> America must translate its well-founded alarm about crime into social actions that will prevent crime. It has no doubt whatever that the most significant action that can be taken against crime is action designed to eliminate slums and ghettos, to improve education, to provide jobs, to make sure that every American is given the opportunities and freedoms that will enable him to assume his responsibilities.
>
> (quoted by Caplan 1973: 591)

Its remedies inevitably pointed to extra government inter-vention and welfare expenditure which even then seemed to be providing only minimal solutions to such problems.

All that then seemed to happen in the shift from welfar-ism to neo-liberalism that took place around 1980 was that governments, instead of ineffectively trying to resolve such problems themselves, now attempted to transfer ownership of them back onto local communities in what Garland (2001) refers to as a series of 'responsibilization' strategies – encouraging investment in crime prevention technologies, safer community councils and so on. Even the police, despite being the recipient of the extra powers, resources and pay derived from earlier law and order campaigns, confirmed that parts of the crime problem were beyond their capabil-ities to resolve. Hence the New Zealand Police Commis-sioner's comments that 'New Zealand was becoming a more violent society and there was little the police could do to stop that' (*The Dominion* 27 August 1994: 3).

When there is no belief that governments and the crimi-nal justice authorities still have the solutions to such prob-lems, then vigilantism becomes a possible response. This is a form of political action designed not to subvert the existing social order but instead to sustain it at exactly the time that the authority of the central state is either too weak or too exhausted to do so itself (Johnston 1996). The vigilante activities that have increasingly come to prominence in Britain and New Zealand from the early 1990s (see, for example, Girling *et al.* 1998) are further evidence of the extent to which trust in the political establishment has broken down. However, a much larger body of citizens, not sufficiently distanced from the authorities to be prepared to forcibly take law enforcement into their own hands, but sufficiently distanced from them to be disillusioned and dis-trustful, and no longer having an affiliation determined at birth to one mainstream political party or another, will be more likely to put their trust and support in those populist organizations and political movements which claim to have solutions to rising crime and various other hitherto irresolvable problems: magical, commonsensical solutions usually based on invocations of a golden time when social stability and order was unquestioned. Right-wing commentator Richard North (2003: 1) thus writes nostalgically that:

> [W]ithin my lifetime this society knew a coherence which has gone. It united classes and regions and generations. Broadly speaking, there was agreement about various things which mattered a good deal. These included ideas about public behaviour . . . about holding the monarchy and parliament in a degree of awe; about respect for authority in general . . . about believing the Civil Service was fair. There was respect for learning and in particular academic authority.

At the same time, when many other aspects of life have become unfamiliar and unsettling, and beyond the abilities of both individuals and governments to resolve, crime problems at least would seem to have obvious causes and solutions – hence the particular prominence these receive in populist discourse.

However, Tyler and Boeckmann (1997) argue that the growth of punitive sentiments should be seen as a characteristic of more general concerns about a perceived decline in *social cohesion*, rather than being linked to particular levels of crime. What this means is that such sentiments are not tied instrumentally to punishing criminals but are related to the symbolic use of punishment as a means, and one of the most obvious and immediately available means, of restoring order and authority at a time when these qualities have been unravelling right across the social field (Durkheim 1893/1964). By the same token, the more social cohesion seems to be unravelling, the more strident will be the calls for more severe punishments: again, not particularly as a response to crime, which may even be in decline, but as a way of providing consensus and uniformity. This is why, they claim (Tyler and Boeckmann 1997: 256), people in the United States generally support that country's three strikes laws – not because of their fears of crime but because of their perceptions that moral cohesion is deteriorating: 'those citizens who feel that the moral and social consensus that holds society together is declining are more supportive of punitive public policies.'

However, it remains the case that despite falls in recorded crime, despite the drop in the fear of crime amidst indications that some of the precautions against victimization which became second nature in the 1990s are now being relaxed (van Kesteren *et al*. 2000), many people still think that crime is *increasing* (Simmons and Dodd 2003; Ministry of Justice 2003). In these respects, it would surely be mistaken to understate the relationship between penal populism and crime concerns. If most people still think that crime is increasing, even when all the official data points to the opposite, then this rise will be an emblem of the incompetence of the criminal justice establishment. It is also another indicator of the continuing decline of social cohesion and the moral bonds that had previously held society together, and, of course, of the inability of government to arrest this decline. As such, rather than undermining the Tyler and Boeckmann position, increased punitiveness as a reaction *to the perception* that crime remains out of control would seem to strengthen it: it will appear that the criminal law, too, has lost its moral authority.

3

PENAL POPULISM, THE MEDIA AND INFORMATION TECHNOLOGY

Why should people think that crime is increasing when evidence from most modern societies points to its decline? Let us answer this question with another: where do most people get their knowledge of crime from? Two decades after it was made, Wright's (1985: 21) comment that 'for most Americans, the media serves as the primary source of information about crime' still seems appropriate and could almost certainly be generalized to include most other Western countries. People get their knowledge about crime from this source because, as Christie (2004: 89) has argued:

> [I]t is an essential finding that people do not meet people to the extent they once did. This means increased reliance on the media for describing what happens and what gives meaning to the occurrences. It also means greater dependence on the state to cope with these perceived dangers.

People do not meet other people to the extent they once did because of the decline in organic community life and the growth of a more transient labour force. As a result, know-ledge and understanding of the world is no longer likely to be derived from family members and neighbours as before, but instead from more remote and abstract sources, such as the mass media (Giddens 1990). This certainly means that there will be a greater expectation that the state will resolve such dangers, as Christie suggests: *but when the state seems to be manifestly failing in these matters*, people will look to populist forces beyond it which do promise solutions.

How, though, does the media help to produce such effects? The volume and nature of crime reporting enlarges the dimensions of this problem and increases the immediacy of its threat, making it seem one that is acute, requiring drastic and dramatic action. Changes in the structure of the media, brought about by deregulation and the impact of the new information technology have then accelerated this ten-dency: most certainly in the *popular* media, if not necessarily in the *quality* media. By definition, though, it is the popular media which is most widely read and viewed and which thereby has the capacity to be an important opinion-former, at a time when the opinions of its readership have gained much greater political prominence. In its reporting style, crime analysis becomes personalized rather than statistical-ized, as it privileges the experiences of ordinary people, par-ticularly crime victims, rather than expert abstractions. As a result, *in those societies where these trends are particularly evident*, the possibilities for informed public opinion are greatly diminished. In this way, the commonsensical understand-ings of crime and punishment that permeate the popular media are given authority and prestige. It is doubtless for this reason that senior politicians in Britain now regularly write for the popular rather than the quality press.

Furthermore, if one of the hallmarks of the previous axis of penal power had been the ability of elites to control crime knowledge, the impact of the new information technology has meant that they have lost this power. New and competing understandings of crime and punishment in new sites can be transported around the world, beyond the power and control of elites to arrest, but which are instantly recognizable and understood.

CHANGES IN CRIME NEWS

For much of modern society, life had been characterized by what Giddens (1991: 244) has referred to as 'the sequestration of experience.' That is to say, 'the separation of day-to-day life from contact with those experiences which raised potentially disturbing existential questions – particularly experiences to do with sickness, madness, criminality, sexuality and death.' Indeed, as most people in modern society became increasingly uncomfortable in dealing with these aspects of everyday life, so they were steadily hidden away behind bureaucratic screens, to be administered by experts of one kind or another. During the course of the twentieth century, however, most people also became *vicariously* informed about these phenomena as a result of the way in which an ever-expanding mass media relayed information to them – particularly information about crime. This was because crime had become a central part of its staple diet: the reporting of crime is inherently able to 'shock, frighten, titillate and entertain' (Jewkes 2004: 3), sustaining public appeal and interest, selling newspapers and increasing television audiences. Furthermore, the way in which crime is used to achieve these ends is by its *selective* rather than comprehensive reporting. That is to say, crime reporting is based on that which will be interesting to the public, which usually means 'something worse than normal, something a little bit different – something bizarre, unusual or something that has affected a lot of people. Not burglary and things that happen every day' (Allison 1991: 100). Here, then, are likely to be the sources of those 'feelings and intuitions' which become embedded in penal populism.

By the 1970s, the way in which the media, particularly the popular press at that juncture, shaped, directed and created public knowledge about crime was well documented (Chibnall 1977, Hall *et al.* 1978). At that point there was significantly more crime reporting than had been the case in the pre-war and immediate post-war period (Roshier 1973). Thereafter, from constituting 4 percent of news stories in the press for the period 1939–1967 (ibid.), subsequent studies reveal that the concentration on crime news in the media rose to 6.5 percent at the beginning of the 1980s to 13 percent at the end of that decade (Ditton and Duffy 1983; Williams and Dickinson 1993). The research of Reiner and Livingstone (1997) indicates a similar growth of crime reporting from 1945 to the early 1990s in their samples of quality and popular newspapers. By that date, 21 percent of the news content of the press consisted of crime stories.

However, it is not only that crime reporting has quantitatively increased; there have also been qualitative changes in its reporting: it is prone to focus more extensively on violent and sexual crime than in the past (Ericson *et al.* 1991). For example, Wright (1985: 21) noted that 'a recent review of research about patterns of crime reporting found that without exception, violent individual crimes – particularly murders – are represented disproportionately in news media presentations'; Dorfman *et al.* (1997) found that violence was the single most frequent story topic (usually involving youth) in one week of local news broadcasts on 26 California stations; Mauer (1999: 72) found that 'in the United States, TV coverage of crime more than doubled during 1992–3, while murder coverage tripled during the period.' In addition, much contemporary crime reporting features 'new crimes', especially those which put personal safety and security at risk – road rage, stalking and identity theft for example – with more 'normal crimes' rarely mentioned (see Reiner 2001, Jewkes 2004). At the same time, given that it is usually the most popular newspapers – the tabloid press in Britain – that feature most crime stories (Williams and Dickinson 1993), this thereby ensures that the most usual representations of crime, taking the form of randomized, unpredictable and violent attacks inevitably committed by strangers on 'ordinary people', reach the greatest audience.

To a significant extent, these qualitative and quantitative changes in crime reporting can be attributed to the growing diversity of news sources and media outlets and the simultaneous concentration of ownership in the hands of a few media moguls, who are then able to shape broadcasting and publishing styles to suit their own commercial interests – usually the mass market, rather than less profitable niche markets. State organizations in most modern societies up to the 1980s had enjoyed an almost complete monopoly of television broadcasting. Since then, these have had to compete with expanded terrestrial services run by the private sector in addition to satellite and cable television companies. In Britain, which had just three television channels in 1977, only 18 percent of households received satellite, cable or digital television in 1993; this had risen to 48 percent by 2003, with hundreds of channels available. This diversification of television audiences had been signalled by *The Economist* (5 September 1992: 63), writing on the future of this medium: 'for a clue, look to America. There, the cable television boom of the 1980s reduced the audience share of the big three networks from more than 90 percent to 60 percent of the audience.' Indeed, by 2002, 69.4 percent of households in the United States had access to cable television. Similar patterns are now found in most other Western countries. In New Zealand, there had been only two state owned television channels in 1989. Now there are several more privately owned terrestrial channels as well as satellite television to which, in 2005, 40 percent of households had access.

As a consequence, both television and the press have to be much more competitive than used to be the case. Their programmes have to be packaged in such a way that they become more attractive to viewers than those of their rivals and competitors. They also have to be more attractive to advertisers, on whose revenue all independent broadcasting companies and even some which are state owned,[1] in the aftermath of deregulation and economic restructuring, are dependent. Where state owned broadcasting organizations have been affected in this way, these usually have to find a place in the mass market, rather than rest content with a shrinking quality market. These developments solidify the importance of crime reporting, particularly in the news and current affairs programmes of satellite and private television companies, particularly in those of state broadcasters competing with them. Crime not only helps guarantee them an audience because of its intrinsic attractions, but when entire channels are devoted to news, then always readily available crime news will become a particularly important component (Cumberbatch *et al.* 1995, Dorfman *et al.* 1997).

As a result, if scenes of crime and punishment had previously been 'sequestered' from our experience, then today the quantity and quality of these representations are able to pervade everyday discourse, making crime seem all too prominent and close to us (whatever its real distance), to the point where, as Bauman (2002: 89) has pointed out:

[I]f one judged the state of society after its dramatised representations – not just the proportion of criminals to 'ordinary folk' would appear to exceed by far the proportion of the population already kept in jail, and not only the world as a whole would seem to be divided primarily into criminals and guardians of order – but the whole of human life would seem to navigate the narrow gorge between the threat of physical assault and fighting back the potential attacker.

As a demonstration of the power that sections of the popular media can have to define crime control issues and galvanise the public into action around them, Thomas (2005: 22, my italics) writes that:

> [I]n 1996 and 1997, the United Kingdom saw a series of popular 'uprisings' directed against sex offenders. A key element in these crowd reactions *was the part played by the press and media reporting of sex crime* and in particular the new role the press appeared to have taken upon themselves, actually to identify and publicise the whereabouts of sex offenders in the community.

However, the most well-known such incident was instigated by the *News of the World*, Britain's most popular Sunday newspaper, in relation to the rape and murder of eight-year-old Sarah Payne in 2000. Against the background of the tragic death of this child and the anguish of her parents, the paper began a 'naming and shaming' campaign with names and photographs of 49 male and female convicted paedophiles (and went on to publish similar details of 200 more). The feature was headlined, 'DOES A MONSTER LIVE NEAR YOU?' and claimed that 'Everyone in Britain has a child sex offender living within one mile of their home' (*News of the World* 23 July 2000: 2). The apparent omnipresence of this reviled group then led the newspaper to campaign for a 'Sarah's Law', giving rights of notification and warning to local communities if convicted sex offenders were moving to their neighbourhoods. It would be the British equivalent of Megan's Law in the United States, thereby memorializing Sarah, while protecting similar children from Britain's many paedophiles. Against significant opposition to its demands from all the main criminal justice organizations as well as senior government ministers (a rare display of such unity since the rise of penal populism), the newspaper reduced the complex issues associated with community notification to a commonsensical reification of its necessity, as in the following headlines:

Q: 'Would you want to be told if a predatory paedophile lived next door to you?'

A: 'If you say Yes, then you back Sarah's Law. If you say No then you are a LIAR'

(*News of the World* 16 November 2000, quoted by Evans 2003: 185)

By representing the issues in this way, it was as if those who opposed the level of community notification that was being demanded could only be apologists for the paedophiles – there could be no other legitimate reason for their opposition to the paper's proposals.

As it was, the campaign did eventually achieve some measure of success in facilitating more public involvement in the decision-making processes related to sex offenders:

[T]he Government announced that members of the public [would] for the first time be given a direct role in drawing up risk assessment plans and monitoring the thousands of paedophiles and other serious criminals released from prisons each year by taking a place on Multi-Agency Pubic Protection Panels.

(ibid.: 169)

However, the newspaper's exposés also proved to be the catalyst for wide ranging vigilante attacks against paedophiles or suspected paedophiles (Hinds and Daly 2001, Evans 2003). If these attacks demonstrate how fragile the authority of the central state has become, they are also a demonstration of the power of those sections of the media which place themselves unequivocally on the side of 'the people' and against the establishment to challenge and even temporarily usurp this authority.

The way in which *the punishment of crime* is reported further undermines respect for the criminal justice establishment and the authority of the state. This follows much the same course as the reporting of crime itself. Ashworth and Hough (1996: 779) thus write that:

> [M]edia reporting is inevitably selective: news values favour the surprising or frightening or outrageous rather than the mundane and this ensures that the court stories carried . . . are scarcely representative of everyday sentencing practice . . . there is a wide disparity between the newspaper coverage of sexual and violent offences and their lowly place in crime statistics.

This then informs the widely held view that the courts are too lenient, even when they have become considerably more punitive, in addition to the widely held view that crime is continuously increasing when it is in fact falling. In these respects, news reports are likely to concentrate on the ineptitude of criminal justice officials rather than their successes.[2] The reporting of prison conditions, for the most part at least, will confirm already existing public impressions that prison life is an entirely comfortable experience. An article in one of New Zealand's leading newspapers on conditions in that country's prisons concluded that, 'count in the free meals and toiletries, spare time, no responsibilities, computer and gym access, paid part-time work, student loans, sex, drugs and gambling, and suddenly jail does not seem so tough' (*The Dominion Post* 9 April 2005: A8).

In other words, then, in fighting back 'the potential attacker', the impression we gain from much of the media is that we cannot rely on the criminal justice authorities to do this for us – indeed, they seem more preoccupied with furthering the interests of our assailants. Hence the attention we are prepared to give to those politicians and populist organizations who do recognize these threats, who do seem prepared to break through official obfuscation and equivocation, who seem to show strength rather than ineptitude.

THE GLAMOURIZATION OF BROADCASTING

The changing quality and quantity of crime reporting is also a product of what might be termed the *glamourization of the media*. Before this, and in much the same way that the 'Platonic guardians' controlled the development of penal policy in the post-war period, so too similar guardians imposed their own standards and values on the rest of society in the early days of television – and by so doing became the unchallenged and largely unquestioned opinion formers of the day. The BBC programme *The Brains Trust* provides a good example. Beginning on the radio in 1941 then moving to television in the 1950s, a panel consisting of four 'cerebrals', rather than celebrities, provided answers to questions that listeners, then viewers, had sent to them. Professor A. J. Ayer, on being invited to participate in 1956, wrote that his co-panellists were:

> Noel Annan, the Provost of Kings College, Cambridge and not, I think, yet ennobled, John Betjeman, the poet . . . and Donald Tyerman who was editor of *The Economist*. The question master was Norman Fisher who had at that time some position in the Coal Board but later moved into publishing.[3]

The questions that were selected for them tended to raise, in a philosophical manner, 'concrete or abstract issues of morality' (ibid.). At the same time, controversial issues were 'off limits', as was any political partisanship, to ensure that the programme provided viewers with information and opinion that was both pitched at a 'highbrow' level and which also appeared to be objective and impartial. The result of programmes such as this was, as Delli Carpini and Williams (2001: 164) write, 'the elevation and celebration of that which was enjoyed by elites and a parallel devaluation of "the popular".'

At the same time, news reporting tended to be based around 'events' rather than the personality of the journalist covering the story. When journalists did become well known (as happened to a number of wartime correspondents):

> [T]hey carried with them a sense of authority . . . rather than sheer celebrity or the spill-over importance they got by being assigned to a major beat like the White House. Their audience could assume that whatever these figures turned their attention to was important and worthy of attention by the public as a whole.
>
> (Fallows 1997: 54)

Their authority gave the news its importance, not the way it was packaged or presented. By the same token, the concentration of government-owned television stations and the much more limited impact of commercial television maintained this emphasis on factual reporting and objectivity. There was little by way of competition for viewers, nor, because of unproblematic state subsidies, were there any concerns about having to attract more viewers to keep advertisers satisfied with audience ratings. Thus, in relation to the United States:

> CBS's documentaries made little money for the network but enhanced its reputation for seriousness. Government licensing regulations required networks and local stations to devote a certain number of hours each week to public service programming . . . through this period, the news divisions were

subsidized by the rest of the network. Their non-profit existence meant that they always lacked money, but with the money they did have they were more or less free to do as they chose.

(ibid.: 55)

However, subsequent deregulation and technological change has created an environment 'that now seems increasingly incompatible with the structures and practices that maintained the news-entertainment distinction for most of this century' (Delli Carpini and Williams 2001: 162). This has had particularly dramatic consequences for the presentation of news and current affairs on television: essentially, the time allotted to news items has been reduced while their contents have been simplified into easily digestible headlines.[4] Cook (2002: 140–1) thus writes that:

[T]his faster paced news is cheaper to produce requiring less time per item and so less research and background information, and appeals to advertizers who prefer fast paced programmes on many subjects rather than one consisting of lengthy analysis of fewer issues.

Atkinson (1993: 11) describes the impact of these changes on current affairs programmes: 'the essential shift has been away from thematic narrative frames to more episodic and personalized story telling with built in moral viewpoints.' In relation to the United States' CBS flagship current affairs programme, *Sixty Minutes*, Fallows (1997: 57) found that:

[O]f the nearly 500 stories between 1990 and 1994, more than one third were celebrity profiles, entertainment industry stories, or exposés of . . . petty scandals. Barely one fifth of the stories concerned economics, the real workings of politics, or any other issue of long-term significance.

In this way, the distinction between fact and opinion, between public affairs and popular culture and between news and non-news that was presided over and policed by broadcasting elites has been eroded. As a result, 'complex, explanatory narratives are compressed into shorter, instantly understandable messages and pieces of information. Standardized, "informational" knowledge becomes a privileged form of communication, marginalizing alternative styles of expression and unregulated forms of narration' (Franko Aas 2005: 152). In effect, and especially in those societies where deregulation has been most pronounced, primetime viewing, which obviously generates most advertising revenue, must be simplified and made accessible to the widest possible audience: there is then either no funding for programmes that contravene this rule or they are shown off peak. For example, a ten part series, which filmed everyday life in a New Zealand prison, was screened in 2005 on TV1 (the main state channel) at 11.30 pm – with no advance advertising. Furthermore, primetime broadcasting is no longer dependent on journalists with analytical or intellectual skills – indeed, there is no real requirement for these. Instead, to hold public attention, to make programmes attractive to a mass audience, presenters with good looks and celebrity status, often with links to the sports or entertainment industries, are better suited. Indeed, those with purely journalistic skills may find themselves surplus to broadcasting requirements (see Calabrese 2000: 51). In such ways, then, broadcasting has become glamourized – at the same time as its programme contents have been simplified.

This has meant that crime and punishment issues are likely to be exaggerated and dramatized in news programmes to capture audience attention; are likely to take the form of in-depth interviews with victims or 'survivors', rather than be framed around the opinion of elite experts; informed discussion is likely to be replaced by some aspect of 'reality television' – where ordinary, everyday people working in the area of criminal justice are shown doing exactly that. Almost always, however, such programmes which are screened in primetime feature the police rather than any other group of criminal justice professionals. They are then filmed doing what the public assume to be their normal work – heroic crime fighting (Doyle 2003): as opposed to the reports of all the other inept crime professionals. Such programmes are then likely to confirm the pre-existing opinions of their viewers on such matters.

In addition, crime 'shows' tend to replace documentaries. The BBC's *Crimewatch* has become one of the most popular such shows on television and numerous other countries now have their counterpart (Jewkes 2004: 153). With the use of dramatic reconstructions and surveillance footage, the programme is designed, on the face of it, to help the police solve crime; its reconstructions are meant, ostensibly, to elicit calls from the public with information and fresh clues. While there is no doubt that it has had some significant successes in this way, there also seems no doubt that its success in generating a large audience has been dependent on its capacity for sensationalizing crime:

> *Crimewatch* prioritises crimes of violence and may amplify public fears that crime is spontaneous, random and indiscriminate. One of the unfortunate consequences of a television programme that relies on audience ratings, not only for its commercial success, but also to justify its self-proclaimed role in the business of crime detection is that the producers actively seek out stories that will capture the public imagination and prick the consciences of any potential informants sufficiently to encourage them to pass on information.
>
> (ibid.: 155)

Because the programme is based on 'real crime', not fiction, the audience's vicarious experience of crime becomes that much closer – hence its intrinsic attraction. At the same time, it offers viewers, if they have information to give to the police, the extra enticement of being able to participate in solving the crime (from the security of their own home) *and* appearing on television themselves, when, as with all reality television, they too have fleeting opportunities to become celebrities – just like the programme's presenters. At the same time, the 'realities' of the fictional reconstructions on the programme provide drama and theatre that heighten public anxieties. Meanwhile, there is little recognition that crime is not necessarily the predatory menace that *Crimewatch* reconstuctions make it out to be, nor that its level may have stabilized, may even be receding. Indeed, given the broadcasting structure in which the programme is framed, there *can* hardly be any, since to do so would be to undercut the very premises on which it is based, would undercut the very frames of reference through which viewers have come to know and understand crime through the self-same programmes – which are then able to reconfirm them.

NEW INFORMATION TECHNOLOGY AND DEMOCRATIZATION

As viewer participation in *Crimewatch* also indicates, access to the mass media has been *democratized*. Through the impact of new information technology, ordinary people are increasingly provided with the opportunity to make, report and comment on the news themselves. This ensures that establishment elites no longer have exclusive control of knowledge and information, whether this is about crime or anything else. Use of the Internet, fax, e-mail and videophones 'have dramatically increased the amount and range of information that is readily available, the speed it becomes available and the opportunities for interactive mass communication' (Delli Carpini and Williams 2001: 166). In addition, the development of talk-back radio has accelerated these moves towards mass participation in news making and opinion forming. Such programmes are usually hosted by 'entertainers', rather than journalists, who nonetheless present their shows as legitimate fora for serious consideration of political events and issues. However, unlikely to have specialist knowledge or training themselves, unlikely to have researched the issue in question but relying themselves on newspaper headlines for their leads, they are likely to fall back on commonsense as a way of understanding these matters and by so doing reaffirm the commonsense world views of their listeners. Not only this, but by the very nature of this medium, authority and stature is then given to callers' opinions – these carry just as much weight as those of any 'experts' who may be interviewed during the course of the programme.

Talk-back began in the early 1960s in the United States. By 1985 in that country, 'there were about 300 commercial stations with an-all-talk format; today there are upwards of 1,100 . . . One out of five adults in the country listen regularly; in a 1993 poll of listeners 36 percent said it was their favourite source of political information' (*The Nation* 10 April 1995: 482). Australian estimates indicate that talk-back stations there claim between one-third and one-quarter of total radio audiences (Ward 2001). Even BBC Radio, while not relinquishing elite presentations such as its famous annual Reith lectures, has a talk-back element. 'Straw Poll', for example, is 'a debate programme addressing topics of abiding interest.' Its presenter states that:

> I think what makes Straw Poll distinctive is the variety of ways in which Radio 4 listeners can participate. Members of the audience at the programme can interact with the panellists

> and vote at the end. The nationwide telephone vote is highly
> impressive.
>
>   (www.bbc.co.uk/radio4/news/strawpoll.shtml)

Overall, the growth and popularity of this medium is
indicative of the way in which ordinary people want to be
involved in opinion forming themselves, rather than allowing elites to do this for them; want to give their views and
expect them to be respected, rather than deferring to those of
elites.

Furthermore, in this new democracy, information can be
immediately transmitted by anybody and is available to
everybody. Politicians are able to converse more directly
with 'the people', without this being filtered through a
range of civil service intermediaries. In Britain, it is now
possible to e-mail the Prime Minister's Office, or log on to
the Downing Street webpage; in 2003 the Labour government launched another electronic initiative inviting the
public to participate in the Prime Minister's 'Big Conversations' with the British people (Ryan 2004). In countries such
as Australia and New Zealand, politicians feature regularly
on talk-back radio – indeed, one even had his own show
while serving as a Cabinet Minister.

By making use of these new possibilities of communication, populist law and order groups have been able to gain a
much greater prominence for their views, while most of
their opponents have remained silent, whether this has been
by choice, in the case of most academics, or by compulsion
in the case of civil servants and judges. In New Zealand, the
first page of the SST's website includes the following
statement:

> The [SST] was formed in March 2001 by a small group of
> motivated people with a passion and a vision to help create a
> patriotic, crime free New Zealand through the promotion of

personal responsibility and a better deal for Victims of crime
... The Trust encourages our members to become pro-active
ambassadors by educating their respective communities as to
the horrific consequences and ongoing effects of violent crime,
for those directly involved and the wider community.

(www.safe-nz.org.nz, my italics)

The page contains a 'Victim memorial' (for victims of violent crime 1980–2005) and provides details of the murder of a 15-year-old girl and the assault on the mother of Norm Withers, which had prompted him to organize the 1999 referendum; there is also a changing tally to count the number of murder victims in 2006. In addition, it has released a CD entitled *Enough is Enough*. In such ways, while it advertises itself as the (self-appointed) representative of crime victims, it also claims to speak on behalf of the wider community since each member of it has the potential to become a crime victim. While there may well be other voices offering very different views on crime and punishment, by its astute use of media opportunities, this organization has become '*the voice of the people*' on these issues, consulted by politicians[5] and courted by the media for opinion and comment. Indeed, its spokespeople here and elsewhere are gifts for journalists because of the way in which they present them with headline features and opinion. And because of the high profile they then gain, these spokespeople, who always seem available for these purposes (unlike most elite commentators) become just as authoritative if not more so than 'out of touch', discredited patrician experts.[6]

The successes of Norm Withers in New Zealand and Mike Reynolds in California are specific examples of the way in which those who claim to speak for 'the people' are given this authority and status. Unlike establishment experts, the knowledge that they were professing while campaigning for support for their respective referendum and ballot drew on personal experience, commonsense and anecdote rather than social science research, and newspaper headlines rather than detailed analysis of crime patterns. As Withers stated in the course of one interview:

> *You read the papers every day, look what's happening.* Its time to toughen up so we can deter [criminals] from wanting to go back to prison. These do-gooders and civil libertarians who want to look after the well-being of criminals, its time they got real and thought about the victims.
>
> (*The Dominion* 1 January 1999: 2, my italics)

As a result of the attention given to them, they were able to rearrange the terms of penal debate: policy was judged on the basis of sentence length, deterrence and satisfaction to victims, rather than financial cost, effectiveness as measured by reconviction rates and humanitarianism. In such ways, they were able to provide a steady critique of *bête noire* liberal policies, institutions and professions. Their campaigns thus had a twofold edge. The desire for longer, more punitive prison sentences was inextricably linked to the desire to curtail the power and authority of those members of the establishment who seemed to want to defend the criminal rather than protect innocent victims. For Reynolds, his opponents were 'weird ducks and blind fools' and, probably worst of all, 'ultraliberals', by now a particularly telling condemnation:

> [W]hile crime was *the* center-stage political issue in 1994, it was also emblematic of something far larger: the codification of 'liberal' as a dirty word, the emergence of right wing talk radio as a major political force, and the realignment of American politics, so that henceforth the game would be played with the conservatives playing offense.
>
> (Domanick 2004: 139)

It was establishment liberals who had been associated with unwanted leniency in sentencing and the opaque nature of the punishment process, where 'life' did not mean life and where there was no 'truth in sentencing.' Similarly, in New Zealand, Withers explained in one of his press conferences that:

> Discretion, in my opinion, brings in too many elements of soft-ness. If you do the crime, you do the time . . . I point the finger at the judges on that one. If we leave it to their discretion it will become a joke. There's too much discretion. I'm trying to avoid the mockery of the system . . . The current system is a joke anyway. Life means about thirteen or fourteen years, if that. If they say life, it should be life.

> (*The Dominion* 1 January 1999: 2)

They exposed the threat of crime and the incompetence of the criminal justice authorities – unlike criminal justice experts who tried to *explain* crime and rationalize responses to it. In such ways, they provided a direct source of energy for penal populism by building an unbridgeable gulf between the public and the authorities, presenting the former as always dissatisfied and cheated, and the latter as always distant and ineffective.

VICTIMIZATION AND THE DESTATISTICALIZATION OF CRIME

As democratization has provided the opportunity for the emotive experiences and opinions of ordinary people rather than detached objective expert analysis to become the framework through which crime is understood, victimiza-tion has come to be regarded as a particularly authentic expression of this mode of knowledge:[7] especially when there is an 'ideal victim' who can then become an idealized victim, one who is completely innocent and defenceless, the personification of all that is good and innocent, victimized by another or others who, in the light of such innocence, can only be the antithesis of their victim, can only be utterly malevolent and irredeemable.[8] And the harm they have inflicted on their victim(s) is then seen as harm inflicted on the rest of society, justifying the much greater penal severity that spokespeople for such victims demand.

Polly Klaas became one such victim; and it was as a result of public identification with her that the California three strikes proposal was balloted.[9] As we have seen, the ballot story did not begin with her but with the eighteen-year-old daughter of Mike Reynolds, its organizer. She was murdered in 1992 by a man with a record of drug crime and theft but not violence. She was out with a boyfriend when she was mugged. For trying to hold on to her purse she was shot through the head. It was after this that Reynolds began to collect the signatures he needed for his three strikes proposal to go on the California state ballot, in the hope that its 'street cleaning' effects, to use his own phrase, would permanently incapacitate and neutralize the kind of recidivist criminals responsible for her death. Nonetheless, at the time of the murder of 12-year-old Polly Klaas in 1993, he had gathered only 20,000 of the almost 385,000 signatures he needed for its approval (Domanick 2004: 124). However tragic the murder of Reynolds' own daughter had been, perhaps such an incident was simply too commonplace to raise much public interest. However, after the raped and murdered body of Polly Klaas was found two months after she had been kidnapped from her home, it was this *second* murder, *not the murder of Reynolds' own daughter*, that provided the additional momentum necessary to gather the requisite number of signatures. As Domanick (ibid.: 116) notes:

> Klaas was an innocent. A sweet-faced twelve-year-old suburban

white kid – 'America's child' as *People* magazine would later dub her. Her surreal abduction tapped into every parent's deepest fear and into the public's thirst for twenty four hour a day soap operas.

As such, she was no longer just another 'missing child', just another statistic. She became, instead, *America's innocent child*. The search for her became a nationwide cause, promoted by the media, with added interest for the public because of celebrity involvement in the search for her.[10] Furthermore, she became the first missing child whose story was carried on the Internet, thereby demonstrating the way in which the new information technology had the power to transform such incidents from purely local to national and international tragedies.

After the discovery of her body, Reynolds elicited the support of her father, Mark Klaas, for his ballot. This brought further publicity and predictable results. ' "Polly's death", declared the *Los Angeles Times*, "had bruised the psyche of a nation." CNN and local television stations broadcasted her funeral service live as a message of condolence from President Clinton was read' (ibid.: 126). However tragic and undeserved Kimber Reynolds' death had been, that of Polly Klaas had been turned into something much more than the death of a daughter. The media had transformed her into a national icon of innocence and vulnerability. By virtue of the association Reynolds had been able to establish with her and her father (to the point where, remarkably, the death of his own daughter seemed to largely disappear from the news story), his own crime control initiative was now perceived as necessary to prevent future tragedies of this kind, a strategy so obvious in its simplicity that it was almost beyond any kind of analytical questioning and interrogation (Zimring 1996).

Local and federal politicians thus gave their support to

three strikes laws. Similarly, President Clinton invited Reynolds to the White House (although *not* Mark Klaas). By this time, his ballot had gained an unstoppable momentum. It did not matter that Klaas had now resiled from what Reynolds was hoping to achieve and, with his own father, was actively campaigning against the proposal. For them, the focus should only have been on violent offenders and on 'paedophiles and psychopaths who need to be taken out of society, [and] not on people born into poverty and recycled into the prison system for their entire lives' (ibid.: 134). Klaas had now not only lost his daughter; he had also lost a father's exclusive ownership of the memory of her, as this had become a kind of easily accessible public property: on the Internet, talk-back radio, television chat shows and so on, so skilfully had the murder of Polly Klaas been harnessed to Reynolds' campaign for support for his ballot.

In such ways, the democratization of the media has made it possible for anecdote and personal experience, for talk-back radio hosts who highlight the incompetence of the authorities' responses to crime to become cues for developing policy, independent of the reality of crime and punishment itself. In effect, in those sections of the media 'whose aim is simply to engage our emotions, . . . [so that] "the personal" obliterates "the political" as a factor for human behaviour' (Bird 2000: 225), attempts to discuss crime on the basis of abstract statistics and crime rates are *ipso facto* discredited: 'how do you use statistics and ratios when you're dealing with human lives?', explained a victim in one of the numerous appearances he made on television chat shows in the United States as a consequence of the status this experience had given him (see Anderson 1995: 202). Indeed, as the interviewee intimated, citation of criminal statistics had become a code for softness on crime and callousness towards its victims (ibid.).

The reliance of such personal accounts to establish the

reality of crime effectively 'destatisticalizes' understandings of it: statistics as an authentic measurement and indicator become only one source of information amongst many others the media can draw on in creating its own belief system about crime, but one which is also likely to be the least memorable and the most discredited. Why believe crime statistics, when their evidence is at odds with what the public know about it (usually on the basis of watching, reading and listening to respective media outlets)? As a consequence, populist politicians choose to rely on this public knowledge of crime – it is this knowledge which supersedes any validity that might be found in statistical patterns and trends.[11]

GLOBALIZATION AND SLOGANIZATION

However, the impact of the new technology and the growth of the mass media does more than change the way in which issues of crime and punishment are addressed and made understandable to the public. In just the same way that financial transactions across the globe can be conducted by pushing a button, so too can new ways of thinking about crime and reacting to it be transported around the world. And because of the nature of most crime reporting, this helps to confirm commonsensical beliefs that crime seems to be an imminent threat everywhere, even when research provides statistical data suggesting that local neighbourhoods may be comparatively safe (van Kesteren *et al.* 2000). In such ways, the globalization of crime knowledge of this kind further undermines social cohesion and security, and creates the conditions in which populist forces can thrive.

It has also been the globalization of knowledge that allowed the template for electoral success, patented by Bill Clinton, to be transported around a range of Western countries. The origins of the template are to be found in the 1988 United States presidential election campaign. The

Republican candidate, George Bush (senior), was trailing badly in the polls to Democrat candidate Michael Dukakis, Governor of Massachusetts. At that point, a black murderer named William ('Willie') Horton killed again while on prison furlough from a Massachusetts prison. He came to embody the public's fears of crime, fears of black crime in particular and anger that the liberal establishment could jeopardize the safety of the public by granting him and his kind early release (Anderson 1995, Newburn and Jones 2005). These issues then featured in Bush's advertising campaign and almost certainly won the election for him. For example:

> A grainy photo of Willie Horton was . . . shown and the audience is told that 'despite a life sentence, Horton received ten weekend passes from prison.' The words 'kidnapping', 'stabbing' and 'raping' then appeared on the screen. The ad finished with a photo of Dukakis as the announcer intoned 'weekend prison passes. Dukakis on crime.'
>
> (Newburn and Jones 2005: 76)

Bush had succeeded in making Dukakis, governor of the state where Horton had been imprisoned, appear personally responsible for his release. At the same time Dukakis was never able to shake off this impression during the campaign, relying as he did on technocratic detail to establish his credibility with the electorate, while completely ignoring the symbolic appeal that the Bush campaign carried (Newburn 2002).

As Baker and Roberts (2005: 123) have suggested, 'faced with electorates who are both highly sophisticated consumers of the advertising industry and lacking in time and attention to digest communications of any length, populist politicians can attempt to tailor their message by reducing relevant policies to shorthand form.' Here, then, with perfectly crafted symbols, an incontrovertible link had been established between Horton's crimes and Dukakis' elitist liberalism, confirming the public's suspicions of such qualities and thereby undermining the latter's electoral platform. It also demonstrated the power of this symbolism, the depth of public anxieties about such matters and the need for politicians to assure the public that they were responsive to their concerns.

Thereafter, politicians such as Dukakis who lack such communication skills seem destined to be losers. The importance of appearing tough on crime (and thereby not a privileged member of the discredited and distrusted establishment) was acknowledged by the next (successful) Democratic candidate Bill Clinton in 1992. To ensure that he would not be outflanked by his Republican opponents as his predecessor had been, he made a great play of authorizing an execution warrant during his election campaign in 1992 in his role of Governor of Arkansas. By giving out such assurances to the public that he was at one with their expectations and aspirations rather than those of liberal elites, he became a political winner. He then helped to ensure his re-election in 1996 with similar gestures – making sure, for example, he was identified with the Megan's Law supporters. Furthermore, as he presided over the country's spiralling prison population,[12] this now became an emblem of political strength, not shame or incompetence, providing him with a cast iron defence against any accusations from his opponent that he was not tough enough on crime. In such ways, and in contrast to Dukakis, he became a winner, as have successive left-leaning politicians who have since followed in his footsteps.

Of course, the subsequent penal strategies that they have pursued differ between themselves and from the United States. As Newburn and Jones (2005: 74) note in relation to Britain and this country:

> [While] there have been close parallels in the media and polit-
> ical rhetoric concerning the risk posed by paedophiles, includ-
> ing campaigns for public notification schemes for sex offenders,
> ... the degree to which this rhetoric has been played out in
> concrete changes in policy has been strikingly different in the
> two countries.

Indeed, penal populism does not take the form of an exact
blueprint. There are certainly common themes associated
with it, as it moves from country to country as we have seen;
but as we have also seen, the form it takes is very much
dependent on local contingencies and the opportunities
which local circumstances present, as would be expected in
any political force driven more by emotion than rationality.
The essential point, though, is that despite subsequent
policy differences, politicians voicing the slogans associated
with this rhetoric which has travelled around the modern
world – 'Life means Life', 'Three Strikes', 'Zero Tolerance'
and so on – are sowing the seeds for the growth of penal
populism in their country, even if its subsequent harvest
is likely to differ in shape and form. As Franko Aas (2005:
159) suggests:

> [A] good slogan presents a message or a theme that has instant
> meaning and appeals to the audience. The messages that slo-
> gans contain can 'travel' and are universal in their application
> regardless of the constraints of time and space. Politicians in
> Oslo, for example, talk of 'zero tolerance', sometimes without
> even feeling the need to translate the message.

There is no need to translate the message, and anyway, neither the public receiving it, nor those sections of the media
delivering it want literal translations, with background
information, statistics, strengths and weaknesses and so on
as proof of its affectivity. The message is already understood,

and no elitist expert pointing to downward trends in the crime statistics can interrupt it. The meaning of such messages is in the rallying call they constitute for citizens across modern societies who feel that they have been left vulnerable and unprotected as the world they used to know has collapsed all around them; the rallying call they constitute for action which demonstrates that 'the people' will no longer tolerate any further loosening of those bonds that had successfully been able to hold society together in the past, but which the liberal establishment, typified by its responses to crime, has allowed to fragment.

4

PENAL POPULISM AND CRIME CONTROL

Towards the end of the twentieth century, a clear pattern seemed to be emerging in crime control policy in modern society. On the one hand, the state had been prepared to respond to concerns about monstrous criminals and demonic others with increasingly severe penalties; on the other, there was a strategy of 'defining deviance down', by incorporating 'a criminological perception that viewed the criminalization of minor deviations as unnecessarily stigmatizing and counter productive' (Garland 2001: 117–18). The appropriate response to these 'minor deviations' took the form of diversion, cautions and so on – in effect, reacting to them as a common-place unproblematic aspect of everyday life. However, the rise of penal populism has led to a reorganization of this carefully modelled bifurcation. In contrast to this, crime control policies influenced by penal populism are more likely to reflect opportunity and contingency, and are designed to have purchase with its constituency of 'ordinary people' and their anxieties and fears.

What this has then meant is that the punishment of the monstrous, particularly those who commit sexual crimes against the young, has become significantly more severe, as liberal restraints that might previously have blocked such tendencies have been pushed aside. At the same time, 'minor deviations' are no longer 'defined down'. Instead, a range of groups who fall within this category – young offenders, persistent offenders and a diverse cohort made up of those who may only have displayed 'incivilities' rather than committed crimes – have become urgent priorities for law enforcement, also demanding maximum rather than minimum responses from the criminal justice authorities.

This new pattern in crime control policy is particularly characteristic of Britain and the United States. However, there are inevitably local differences where penal populism influences policy development (see above). This is evident in relation to drug crime (*contra* Bottoms 1995, Roberts *et al.* 2003). In Sweden, Denmark and the Netherlands (see Tham 2005, Balvig 2005, van Swaaningen 2005), there has been a crackdown, largely as a reaction against the tolerant approach taken to this issue in these countries in the recent past: the visible presence of drug addicts in these countries had become a symbol of misplaced welfarism and tolerance, now thought to be corroding their economic and social fabrics. In contrast, in Britain and New Zealand, two countries where penal populism has been very influential, drug concerns have been much less visible: even in the United States, these have been somewhat muted elements in the three strikes movement.

The reasons for the differences would seem to be that in the latter three countries *there was no recent history of tolerance* that penal populism could react against. The 'war on drugs' in the United States has been a reflection not so much of clear, voluble voices *from the public* characteristic of penal populism, but instead of that earlier form of populism where politicians alone spoke on behalf of 'the silent majority'. The whole point about penal populism is that this 'majority' is no longer silent. When it does speak about crime, it has not really prioritized drug use, as the opinion poll evidence provided by Roberts *et al.* (2003) makes clear. Instead, for many people, intermittent experience with soft drugs has become 'a normal part of the leisure-pleasure landscape' (Parker *et al.* 1995: 25) – it is not beyond their experience, not beyond the possibilities of participation for them. This seems likely to be the reason for the success of citizens' ballots in California prescribing mandatory treatment and rehabilitation for drug offenders in that state rather than imprisonment. These measures have provided the first inroads to its hitherto impregnable three strikes law (Domanick 2004). Importantly, crime control policy driven by penal populism targets 'others', not ordinary, 'normal' people.

SEX CRIMINALS

For these same reasons, sexual predators in the United States, paedophiles in Britain, have come to be seen as iconic emblems of evil, hunting and stalking their innocent victims. Driven animalistically by their sexual impulses, it seems, they necessitate special measures of control and containment. The United States sexual predator laws, prescribing criminal detention followed by civil confinement, are thus justified on the basis that they address the irredeemable menace such criminals are thought to pose. As Vachss (1993:1) has commented:

> [N]one can be rehabilitated, since they cannot return to a state that never existed. The concept of coercive therapy is a contradiction; successful psychiatric treatment requires participation, not mere recipients. What makes sexual predators so intractable and dangerous is that they like what they do and want to keep doing it.

Indeed, all the indications in the United States are that the drive against child sex offenders is becoming more intense and exclusionary, with the adaptation of 'one strike' laws in some jurisdictions. As Governor of California Arnold Schwarzenegger explained when giving his backing to that state's Sexual Predator Punishment and Control Act in 2005, 'that means no excuses, no second or third chances in order to hurt others. You do this one time, you go in for life.'[1]

In Britain, a 'two strike' sentencing process, introduced in the Crime (Sentencing) Act 1997, was targeted at paedophiles and justified by New Labour Home Secretary Jack Straw on the basis that 'there is a group of dangerous and severe personality disordered individuals from whom the public at present are not properly protected, and who are restrained effectively neither by the criminal law nor by the provisions of the Mental Health Act' (quoted by Thomas 2005: 120). This has since been repealed by the Criminal Justice Act 2003 which puts their punishment on a 'one strike' footing, with provisions for extended and indeterminate sentences. In addition, in both jurisdictions there is the range of community notification processes awaiting them if and when they are released. Even so, for many people, these measures of control and surveillance are not enough. As vigilante attacks in Britain have demonstrated, many people simply want *the complete expulsion* of these individuals. Their presence in a local community has become intolerable. Roberts *et al.* (2003: 166) thus quote one Brighton mother talking about a local paedophile as follows: 'this man must go. I don't care where he goes to as long as he goes away from here.'

Of course, special measures to control dangerous sex offenders had been in existence in these and other common law jurisdictions for much of the twentieth century – the sexual psychopath laws in the United States, the sentence of preventive detention in Britain, and the equivalent of this indefinite prison sentence in similar anglophone countries (see Pratt 1998). However, around 1970, most had been repealed or had fallen into disuse (Bottoms 1977). It had become clear by then that these special powers offended cultural and judicial sensitivities. In the post-war era especially, it was thought measures involving unlimited detention had more resonance with totalitarian rather than democratic societies. In these respects, contemporary concerns about such criminals represent something more than a continuance of longstanding hostilities to them. The term 'predator' only entered the United States criminal justice lexicon in 1989 when the first of its sexual predator laws was passed in Washington state; in Britain the term 'paedophile' only assumed similar overtones from 1996 (see Soothill *et al.* 1998, Thomas 2005). At the same time, in the new legislation against sex offenders in Britain and the United States, dangerousness has become a much more normalized legal category, rather than one remaining on the periphery of available sanctions, as had always been the case in the past.[2]

What is it, then, that has brought about this resurgence of hostility and loathing? One straightforward reason is that, given the nature of populism, we should expect that crime control policy will gravitate towards such easy and familiar targets, for whom there is likely to be the least public sympathy, the most social distance and the fewest authoritative voices (if any) to speak on their behalf: those who commit sex crimes against children obviously fall into this category. In addition, sections of the media have raised public concerns as a result of the attention given to a small number of spectacularly horrific crimes. The Washington state legislation was introduced as a reaction to the crimes committed by Earl Shriner on a seven-year-old boy, after being released from prison where he was serving a sentence for a similar offence:

> [I]n prison Shriner had designed a van that he reportedly proposed to use for abducting, torturing and killing children, and

corrections officials knew this. Nonetheless, he was released. The question was why an offender was released into the community when so much evidence showed that he was both able and eager to do further harm.

(Jenkins 1998: 36)

The reporting of similar cases thereafter 'raised the spectre of the predator criminal from a minor character to a common, ever-present image' (Surette 1994: 132). Indeed, it is exactly this kind of knowledge that informs the Governor of New Mexico's 2005 proposals for sexual predators:

[W]e see it in the headlines nearly every day – in Florida, Idaho and across the country, violent sexual predators are destroying the lives of children and terrorizing communities . . . I am proposing legislation that will create life sentences, lifetime parole, and will prevent the worst of the worst from being released and threatening our communities and children. We have made progress in dealing with sexual predators, but it's clear we must go further.[3]

In Britain, contemporary anxieties about paedophiles represent the convergence of disparate concerns about the well-being of children and their security, all vividly reported in the mid 1990s: seemingly lenient sentences for sex offenders; child abuse in children's homes; the Dutroux case in Brussels; Fred West, his wife and their 'house of horrors' in Gloucester; the spree killing of 16 children in Dunblane by a former youth club worker; and the release of mental patients into the community who then became confused with offenders on parole or bail who reoffended.[4] In addition, there was news from the United States about Megan's Law, which not only pointed to a way of giving local communities more involvement in the control of such criminals on release from prison, but also signalled that the authorities should not be trusted with this alone.

However, a new value that became attached to children towards the end of the twentieth century also lies behind these concerns. Mary Douglas (1966: 4) wrote that, in all societies, that which is seen as 'pure' not only conveys a sense of order and rightfulness, it also draws attention to the menace of the pollutants to it: 'for us, sacred things and places are to be protected from defilement. Holiness and impurity are at opposite poles.' Impurities, pollutants and abuses have to be removed and the pursuit of such tasks can then become a way of organizing the social environment: 'ideas about separating, purifying, demarcating and punishing transgressions have as their main function to impose system on an inherently untidy experience' (ibid.). By extension, the greater the investment of purity in a particular object or being, the greater the menace impurities that threaten it are thought to be, and the greater the vigilance that is needed to guard against them.

In contrast to earlier periods in the twentieth century (see Best 1990), children now seem to have been endowed with these values of innocence and purity. As a result, those who endanger them come to be seen as the worst type of pollutant, unreservedly justifying all the new penal measures directed at them that go beyond previously permissible levels of punishment in modern democratic societies. We can see this shift in values reflected in changing attitudes towards the sexual abuse or sexual assault of children. Kempe and Kempe (1978: 43), pioneers in exposing new dimensions of these crimes, simply noted that these might rob their victims 'of their developmentally determined control over their own bodies; and of their own preference, with increasing maturity, for sexual partners on an equal basis.' They played down the effects of a stranger attack: 'fierce admonishment such as "Don't let anyone touch you there!", or "All men are beasts" are at best not helpful' (ibid.: 55). A decade later, however, Bass and Davis (1988: 29) wrote that:

> [T]he long term effects can be so pervasive that it is sometimes hard to pinpoint exactly how the abuse affected you. It permeates everything: your sense of self; your intimate relationships, your sexuality, your parenting, your work life, even your sanity.

While the genealogy of this dramatic change in attitudes towards child sexual assault is complex and multi-dimensional,[5] there would seem to be two particularly salient aspects of it which have helped to position children and their attackers at the opposite ends of Douglas' polarities. First, as we know, family life and all that is expected of it (security, permanence, and support) has been shattered into fragments for many. Amidst the erosion of certainty and security here and elsewhere in the social fabric, it is as if children have been invested with a profound emotional and moral significance. As Furedi (2001: 107) puts the matter:

> [A]t a time when very few human relations can be taken for granted, the child appears as a unique emotional partner in a relationship ... unlike marriage or friendship, the bond that links a parent to a child cannot be broken; it is a bond that stands out as the exception to the rule that relationships cannot be expected to last forever.

Again, though, when children have such a value placed on them, we then become increasingly alert to those who would put this at risk, who would destroy that which has come to be, and which we need to be, inviolable.

Second, in any society, one of the factors that is going to determine the way in which children are valued will relate to their numbers in the population at large. In modern societies, the number of live births has declined from the 1970s to the point where social reproduction is significantly threatened. Simultaneously, average family size has also declined, from, for example, 2.9 to 2.4 in Britain in 2001 (Central Statistical

Office 2002) and 3.58 to 3.14 in the United States from 1970 to 2000 (United States Census Bureau 2001). In effect, children have become increasingly scarce commodities, and the need to protect them from any risks to their well-being can lead to the construction of a much greater degree of protective control and regulation around them (Furedi 2001). However, the same processes that have led to this sanctification of the child also ensure that the firm boundaries of protection that we wish to throw around them have been eroded, often dissolved altogether, making this task more fraught and problematic. This is often due to the more regular 'turnover' of personal relationships, allowing, as it does, strangers to wander in and out of family life. On this, Ulrich Beck poses the following questions:

> Ask yourself what actually is a family nowadays? What does it mean? Of course, there are children, my children, our children. But even parenthood, the core of family life, is beginning to disintegrate under conditions of divorce ... [G]randmothers and grandfathers get included and excluded without any means of participating in the decisions of their sons and daughters.
>
> (quoted by Bauman 2001: 6)

Additionally, changing employment patterns and labour mobility have themselves not only contributed to the scarcity of children in the population (child raising often being deferred in favour of career development) but have also led to a growing reliance on extra-familial child care. Indeed, for many single parents, there is now no choice about working: not simply to fulfil their potential as consuming subjects in market driven societies, but because of economic necessities as solo parents with no local family to assist with child care. Newsom and Newsom's (1963) study of parental care now seems remarkable for its total absence of any consideration of nursery care for preschool children in any families involved

in the research (just a few might occasionally use babysit-
ters to allow the parents to go out in the evening). Thereafter, however, we find increasing and accelerating recourse
to day care beyond the family. In the United States, the
numbers of preschool children enrolled in such *formal* provision (unlicensed childminders in the black economy are
not included) grew from 3.75 million in 1970 to 5.94
million in 1990, reaching 6.58 million in 1999, increasing
overall from 33 percent of this population to 60 percent in
this time (United States Census Bureau 2001: 144). In this
era when children have come to be the object of so much
attention and anxiety, Miller (1990: 18) articulates the
dilemmas that contemporary child care arrangements
produce:

> [D]ecide for yourself what are the possibilities. In California,
> state investigators manage to pay unannounced visits to only
> one third of all licensed day care centres each year ... in
> California alone, at least half a million children are receiving
> care which is unmonitored.

It thus seems that the structure of family life is no longer a
defence or barrier to those who threaten the vulnerability
and innocence of children – the firm boundary line
between the family and the menacing stranger that there
used to be is dissolving. Indeed, current concerns about
internet 'grooming' illustrate how flimsy a defence the
traditional family structure is against predatory strangers
able to blend virtual and real worlds and to move between
the two (As one mother was reported as saying, 'a child on
the Internet could be alone in his bedroom and with a
stranger anywhere in the world, *at the same time*' (*Toronto
Globe and Mail* 5 January 2002: F6, my italics). Furthermore, the paedophile's apparent finesse with the new
information technology only makes them seem more

sinister and cunning: 'at one time he was the stereotype of the "man in the grubby raincoat" hanging around street corners . . . from the 1970s [he has been transformed from a] pathetic, sad individual to today's intelligent, manipulative and dangerous manifestation' (Thomas 2005: 1). Hence the need for the special measures of containment that have been placed on the statute books of Britain, the United States and elsewhere.

Of course, a large body of research (see, for example, Finkelhor 1984) clearly indicates that the main perpetrators of such crimes are much more likely to be members of the child's own family than predatory strangers. Nonetheless, the targeting of those lurking outside its perimeters may result in protective boundaries being thrown around its normative status, however unstable and precarious this has come to be. In these respects, contemporary understandings of the predator and the paedophile are borne out of collective anxieties related to the collapsing of social norms and pillars of support; perversely, the concerns about the loathsome intrusions of these criminals may then help to reinforce such norms and pillars by invoking images of idealized families that they put at risk (Evans 2003).

YOUTH CRIME

In the post-1970s period, juvenile justice policy had been based largely around steering young people away from formal intervention by means of informal warnings and cautions until they effectively 'grew out of crime' (Rutherford 1992). However, this trend has been reversed by new policies which have led to the *adultification* of children and young offenders (Jewkes 2004): rather than allowing them to grow out of crime, it is as if their criminality is already irreparably ingrained and has to be sanctioned. Thus, in the United States:

[D]uring the 1980s and 1990s ... the majority of states and also the federal jurisdiction adopted statutory mechanisms that facilitate the transfer of juvenile offenders to criminal courts ... between 1992 and 1997 no fewer than forty four states and the District of Columbia passed laws making it easier for juveniles to be tried as adults. Once transferred in this way, juvenile offenders are liable upon conviction to be sentenced in the same way as if they were adults sent to the same prisons, and until a Supreme Court decision in March 2005, could even be sentenced to capital punishment for crimes they committed as children.

(Cavadino and Dignan 2005: 217)

Here, then, the barriers that had been steadily set in place over much of the twentieth century to prevent juvenile offenders being further contaminated by any contact with adult penal provisions such as the prison have been increasingly dismantled.

Similarly in England: from 1994 there was an end to the policy of 'caution after caution'. As Home Secretary Michael Howard said, 'from now on your first chance is your last chance. Criminals should know that they will be punished. Giving cautions to serious offenders, or to the same person time and again, sends the wrong message to criminals and the public' (quoted by Newburn 1997: 650). Thereafter, the Home Office (1997) in the White Paper *No More Excuses* – the very title of which reflected this policy reversal – focussed on the 'justice gaps' that diversion, repeat cautioning, delays and inadequate law enforcement had led to and all of which were indicative of a minimal official response to relatively low-level crime (Squires and Stephens 2005). In its aftermath there have been attempts to make juveniles more prosecutable and accountable for their crimes – the age of criminal responsibility has been reduced from fourteen to ten in England.[6] Legislative barriers to keep children and young people out of prisons have also been removed, alongside the introduction of more explicitly punitive sanctions – at a time when, 'far from a youth crime wave being upon us, offending by young people has been *decreasing*' (Cavadino and Dignan 2002: 285; see also Zimring 2005 in relation to the United States). From the 1980s, boot camps, 'involving residential military style training that frequently includes hard physical labour and demeaning verbal degradation' (Cavadino and Dignan 2002: 300) have become an increasingly popular response to juvenile and youth offending in the United States and were briefly replicated in Britain, Australia and Canada in the 1990s. There are also explicitly restrictive sanctions such as night restriction orders in Britain, while in the United States, three quarters of the largest cities have juvenile curfews (Gostomski 1997).

Again, though, while it might be thought that the focus on youth should be of no surprise – young people constitute another easy target and have always been thought to be 'out of control' (Pearson 1983) – there is more to these current concerns than mere opportunism. From the early 1980s, new social divisions, based around categories of inclusion and exclusion (Young 1999), have opened up across modern society, just as the old class divisions were becoming much more fluid and permeable. This experience was particularly acute in Britain which then found itself in the forefront of what became a more general economic reconstruction. The immediate result was the:

> [R]eduction of the primary labour market, the expansion of the secondary market and the creation of an underclass of structurally unemployed . . . the downsizing of the economy involves 'lean production' in manufacturing industry with the de-skilling of labour and the flexibility of the work force.
>
> (ibid.: 8)

These changes in employment patterns became one of the first and most obvious indicators that what had previously been 'normal' and taken for granted was no longer so. In these respects, if those with skills and appropriate levels of education have ultimately been given access to high expectations of material success and self-fulfilment, a small but sizeable segment (thirty percent of the British population was Hutton's [1995] estimate) in a rearranged class structure now found themselves with only a peripheral place in these consumer-driven societies.

Young people leaving school without educational qualifications were hardest hit by these deep structural changes. Indeed, they found themselves in the vanguard of the new excluded class. As Harrison (1983: 125) wrote at the start of this period:

> [N]ever has the gap between youthful desires and reality been wider. Unemployment has hit the young harder than any other age group. The practice of last in first out victimises them. Firms choosing whom to make redundant picked on those with shortest service that would qualify for least redundancy pay, and in choosing whom to take on, prefer the ready trained rather than those they would have to train themselves.

The future for many of them was one of long-term unemployment interspersed with periods of part-time or shift work in one of the new low pay service industries, or periods of government imposed 'training'. In effect, their own horizons were being dramatically narrowed, just as those of the included class were being dramatically widened:

> [O]ne of the commonly offered recommendations to the young . . . is to be flexible and not particularly choosy, not to expect too much from jobs, to take jobs as they come without asking too many questions, and to treat them as an opportunity to be

enjoyed on the spot as long as it lasts rather than as an introductory chapter of a life project, a matter of self-esteem and
self-definition, not a warrant of long-term security.

(Bauman 2004: 72)

It was also clear that the discipline of the labour market
would no longer be sufficient to regulate those who were
only peripherally attached to it. Governments have thus had
to develop additional control strategies for this surplus and
potentially toxic population. In the United States, with only
a minimal welfare structure in existence, this responsibility
has fallen primarily on the police. As regards Los Angeles,
Davis (1992: 286) writes of:

[A] generation under curfew. Vast sections of the region's
sumptuous playground, beaches and entertainment centres
have become virtual no-go areas for young Blacks or Chicanos
... Residential curfews are deployed selectively and almost
exclusively against black and Chicano neighbourhoods ...
Police now have virtually unlimited discretion, day or night, to
target 'undesirables', especially youth.

In Britain, in contrast, its welfare apparatus was redesigned
to provide a similar function. As the transition from school
to work that had been an almost completely unproblematic
event during the post-war period to this point virtually
collapsed, a range of new initiatives now offered more 'training' and (rudimentary) education to provide assistance across
what had suddenly become a particularly problematic phase
in life. This took the form of participation in 'preparation for
life' courses, youth training programmes and 'life and social
skills' courses. The quasi-educational institutions of government that regulated this new sector then came to be
enmeshed within penal and welfare agencies, often with the
same kind of programme being made available for the young

criminal as that which had been set in place for the young unemployed person – creating, overall, a much denser web of social control around youth in general and young offenders in particular (Cohen 1985).

At the same time, the presence of young people such as these in public space became increasingly problematic, prescribed and restricted as public space itself became more commercialized and privatized. The new shopping malls that were being built began to develop their own policing processes to keep them out:

> [A]n ongoing and daily struggle is waged between what are opposed interests and purposes ... Most obviously, security guards, wardens, guides and 'hostesses' monitor the action in the site and reprimand or eject boisterous groups. Additionally, however, control may be exercised through ticket booths permitting only certain people to enter or excluding certain ethnic, racial or economic groups ... benches, tables or other common facilities which permit loitering or any unapproved (read unprofitable) activity by mall users and habitués may be removed.
>
> (Shields 1992: 9)

Furthermore, as property values began to soar for those living on the 'included' side of the new social divisions, so too private sector housing built in its own restrictions in the form of 'gated communities'. As a consequence, the unwanted and the undesirable would increasingly be consigned to (often racialized) ghetto areas and sink estates, those areas described by Campbell (1993: 48) as 'throwaway places', places that had always been:

> [T]he first resort of the poor but which, from the early 1980s, had become increasingly desperate places to live in, starved of resources because of public expenditure restrictions and the

> movement of capital to sites where labour was cheaper and
> expectations lower.
>
> (Young 1999: 20)

For youth in these areas, 'training' would not only fail to
provide most of them with any significant career escape
(Finn 1987), but in addition, by taking place on sites which
had themselves become largely surplus to the needs of the new
consumer driven societies – church basements, warehouses,
disused factories – it was unlikely to offer even a temporary
respite from the increasingly cut off, remote and essentially
excluded sectors of society where they found themselves
marooned – although not exiled.

Because, of course, young people from these areas have
regularly burst through such measures of containment, sometimes in spectacular displays of inner city rioting, in relation
to which Newburn (1997: 646) wrote that:

> [W]hat [such] public disturbances did was allow long-standing
> concerns about young or very young offenders to be dusted
> down, distorted, sometimes exaggerated, and then served up in
> symbolic form via the mass media. Within much of the report-
> ing of the events it was increasingly suggested that the greatest
> scourge of inner-city life was the young criminal, who was so
> prolific in his activities that he, almost alone, was terrorizing
> local communities.

In addition, though, they also brought their incipient
menace out of their own zones of exclusion into what had
become privileged areas of affluence and indulgence: simply
'hanging around' in downtown areas would be demonstration enough of this capacity. Indeed, as the gulf and social
expectations of these two sectors of society widened, so
investigative journalists, in echoes of early twentieth century
accounts of British slum life (see, for example, London 1903),

began to write of the difference and 'otherness' of this sub-strata of humanity (see Campbell 1993). Newspaper reports of young people known as 'Ratboy' and 'Spiderboy' who were responsible for local crime waves (Cavidno and Dignan 2002: 298) seemed to confirm the animalistic traits and distinctive physiognomy of this subclass which had been allowed to drift out of the control of the authorities. The Association of Chief Police Officers, for example, claimed that they were power-less to deal with this group (see Newburn 1997: 647), although this seems to have been based largely on anecdote and assertion, since juvenile crime was falling in the early 1990s.

How could the police be powerless to prevent juvenile crime if it was falling? The answer was that it might be falling as a whole, but it might also be the case, as Home Secretary Kenneth Clark asserted in 1992, that '*a small number of children are committing a large number of crimes*. There is a case for increasing court powers to lock up, educate and train them for their own and everyone else's interest . . . If court powers need to be strengthened or new institutions created, then they will be' (Newburn 1997: 646, my italics; see also Roberts *et al.* 2003 in relation to Australia; van Swaaningen 2005 on the Netherlands, Hogeveen 2005 on Canada). In these respects, squaring the circle around police assertions that juvenile crime was out of control and the evidence of a falling juvenile crime rate ultimately produced the reified persistent juvenile offender:

> [I]f there is a small but growing number of juvenile offenders responsible for many offences . . . it is possible to reconcile the indisputable fact that the number . . . of known juvenile offenders has fallen over time with the mere speculative asser-tion that the number of offences committed by juveniles has risen.
>
> (House of Commons Home Affairs Committee 1993: 48)

These characteristics of difference and otherness that sections of the youth population were thought to possess were exemplified by the two 10-year-olds sentenced to be detained 'at Her Majesty's Pleasure' (for minimum terms of ten and eight years respectively) for the horrific murder of 2-year-old James Bulger in Liverpool in 1993. Reports of the proceedings made much of the blighted areas and blighted families that the two boys came from, while their cold, staring, unremorseful appearance in court further separated them and their kind from the sensibilities of the aghast, onlooking public at large (Young 1996). Because the age of criminal responsibility was then 14 in England, the prosecution had to prove that they were not *doli incapax*. When the media representations of them (Young 1996, Jewkes 2004) were then set against the innocence of their victim James, this became one more demonstration of how out of touch the criminal process had become with 'the real world'. Indeed, it was as if it represented a system of intervention that seemed to be naively premised on the innocence of youth, whereas the two boys had demonstrated the wickedness and malevolence it was capable of. There had been too many attempts to 'understand' the problems and crimes of young people, so it seemed, while there was not enough condemnation and punishment.[7]

After public outrage at the (apparent) leniency of the sentences of the two child murderers, Home Secretary Michael Howard ordered that they would serve a minimum term of 15 years,[8] thereby demonstrating his preference for public rather than judicial expectations of justice: and then used the Bulger case to order a significant expansion of secure units for 12- to 16-year-olds (Young 1996: 126). In typically populist fashion, policy was being developed on the basis of the *exceptional* rather than the mundane case. In addition, Howard was now having to compete with the Labour Party's new-found toughness on crime. This more punitive approach to juvenile crime marked the start of the law and order bidding war between the two main parties.

The subsequent reforms and retrenchment of punishment in the English juvenile justice system mirrored a similar pattern in the United States where, up to the 1980s, 'the juvenile court [had become] the only major hold out in the law and order revolution . . . a contrast in both rhetoric and behaviour to the spiral of increased incarceration' (Zimring 1999: 261). By this point, however, juvenile justice systems that were prepared to put their trust in discredited social work authorities had only become indicators of the weakened authority of the state. Youth crime in general, including as it did well-known cases of exceptional wickedness and malevolence, demanded more recognizably punitive responses. Hence the residual popularity of sanctions such as the boot camp or its equivalent. The kind of military discipline these embodied seemed to be an obvious commonsensical solution to the aimless sense of dissatisfaction and disconnectedness now surrounding this estranged youth cohort, while invoking memories of that more stable and secure society when service in the forces was commonplace and orders were readily obeyed (Simon 1995). This is how such sanctions 'work', according to populist understandings of the concept, however irrational these might seem according to establishment criteria of reconviction rates, economic cost and so on. These also work in terms of providing a centre of unification for ordinary people against supposedly out of control, different, animalistic sections of the youth population on whom they are to be inflicted.

PUNISHING PERSISTENCE

In Britain, the principle set out by the Court of Appeal in R v Queen (1981)[9] had ended expectations that persistence in crime would be met by an escalation of punishment, at least in relation to adult offending: 'the proper way to look at the matter is to decide on a *sentence which is appropriate for the offence for which the prisoner is before the court.*' This principle was then enshrined in the Criminal Justice Act 1991, itself the product of behind the scenes informal deliberations in establishment circles, even if formal contacts to this effect had been brought to an abrupt halt in the early 1980s. In accordance with the just deserts philosophy which had heavily influenced it, convictions before the present offence should not be taken into account when passing sentence: persistence would bring no additional sanctions. In fact, this legislation proved to be the highwater mark of such elitist liberal influences, since the principles it put into practice were regarded as completely offensive to popular commonsense. This expected that the more one committed crime, the more one would be punished – a law of infinitely expanding punishment, not one of unchanging constancy. Swift retreats from the legislation culminated in the Home Office (1996) reasserting that persistence had to be taken into account when punishing. There was to be no more 'defining deviance down' – levels of punishment had to take into account the distress even comparatively minor crime caused to victims. For example:

> [B]urglars convicted three times would be subject to a minimum sentence yet to be fixed ... domestic burglary is particularly distressing for victims. It involves the loss of property, sometimes of great sentimental value; considerable expense and inconvenience in sorting out the consequences; and perhaps most of all leaves victims with the sense that the sanctity of their home has been violated ... research shows that most burglars are recidivists.
>
> (ibid.: 51)

Thereafter, the Labour government promised to 'get to grips with the one hundred thousand most persistent criminals' while assuring that punishments would become 'progressively more intense for persistent offenders' (Home Office 2001: 8, 20). The Criminal Justice Act 2003 (s.143) thus provides that the court must treat each previous conviction as an aggravating factor.

This intolerance of – often very minor – persistent adult offending seems unique to Britain (Tonry 2004a). Why should this be so? It bears the hallmarks of local contingency and opportunity characteristic of populist influenced policy. First, it was given significant momentum by the reaction to the highly unpopular Criminal Justice Act 1991 which seemed to exemplify the way in which liberal penal theory had become too influential on policy development (Cavadino and Dignan 2002). Second, in taking up these concerns, the notion of the unrepentant persistent offender – particularly burglars and the distress they caused – presented one more easy target for populist politicians: punishing persistence would be another way of reasserting the authority of the criminal law and restoring stability and security, while allowing emotional responses of victims to privilege rational responses of officials to order the punishment of crime. Third, and more generally, punishing offenders more severely each time they come to court fits well with the market-driven society Britain has become, and the calculating, choosing citizen that its system of governance is now based around. Where rewards are very high for those who have made the right choices about the course of their lives, but where sharp declines and severe hardships are always a possibility as a result of unforeseen dangers and risks, there will be little sympathy for those who deliberately, time and again, make the wrong choices in life, particularly when they then endanger the well-being of others, particularly when they make the high premiums now attached to order and security even more precarious.

On this basis, the renewed interest in punishing persistence should be understood as one consequence of the transition from welfare to market driven social arrangements. Opposition to the 1991 Criminal Justice Act proved to be a local catalyst for this in Britain. In those societies where the state, with few exceptions, is prepared to guarantee everyone a chance in life, which promises to assist those who are unable to make the most of their opportunities, then except in only a small number of cases, there will be few final warnings, and little by way of permanent expulsion. In contrast, in a society where everyone must make their own way in the world and make provision for their own misfortunes, there is little by way of social bonds and interdependencies that provide support, especially for the most recalcitrant and troublesome. Punishing persistence in Britain, along with the effects of some of the more broadly drafted three strikes laws in the United States, becomes a way of putting down markers which redefine the boundaries of penal tolerance: there will be none for those who trespass beyond the new limits that have been set.

INCIVILITIES, ANTI-SOCIAL BEHAVIOUR AND 'LACK OF RESPECT'

At the same time, law enforcement has been extended into the policing of behaviours which may not even constitute crime. It had been concerns about 'incivilities' rather than crime itself which lay behind the introduction of 'zero tolerance' policing in New York in the early 1990s. Its author, Chief of Police William J. Brattan (1997: 33) wrote that:

> [I]n the 1970s and most of the 1980s, there was not a subway car in the city that was not completely covered with what some inappropriately described as an aberrant form of graffiti; subway stations [had become] shanty towns for the homeless and aggressive begging increased, exacerbating a climate of fear,

compounded by a significant and notorious decline in the quality of life as a whole.

Skogan (1992: 2) similarly reported in Chicago that disorder, not simply crime, was corroding communities (and involved exactly the kind of activities that the police were then reluctant to become involved with):

> Disorder is evident in the widespread appearance of junk and trash in vacant lots; it is evident too in decaying homes, boarded up buildings, the vandalism of public and private property, graffiti, and stripped and abandoned cars in streets and alleys. It is signalled by bands of teenagers congregating on street corners, by the presence of prostitutes and pan handlers, by public drinking, the verbal harassment of women and open gambling and drug use. What these conditions have in common is that they signal a breakdown of the local social order. Communities beset by disorder can no longer expect people to act in civil fashion in public places.

In Britain, there had been growing concerns in the 1990s about behaviour affecting the quality of life – 'littering', 'flyposting', 'young people hanging about', 'speeding traffic', 'inconsiderate parking', 'fireworks' and 'vandalism and graffiti' (see Mayhew *et al.* 1994, Mirrlees-Black *et al.* 1998). Thereafter, the everyday trespass on ordinary life by 'squeegie merchants', 'addicts', 'winos', 'beggars' and 'neighbours from hell' has become a regular feature of political and popular discourse. The House of Commons Home Affairs Committee (2005: 37) noted that even:

> [A]ctivities such as playing football in the street are not necessarily harmless; persistent use of a garden gate, house wall or car or other inappropriate locations as goalposts – perhaps accompanied by abuse or threat when challenged – can amount

to intolerable behaviour which should not be dismissed by the authorities.

It is conduct such as this, touching on the lives of so many (the House of Commons Home Affairs Committee [ibid.: 8] calculated that there are some thirteen and a half million instances of such behaviour per year, or one every two seconds) which becomes the most obvious signifier of the decline of social cohesion, authority and order. And it is concerns about exactly this kind of conduct that make up much of everyday discourse, distilling as it is probably more likely to do around identifiable and regular local agitation about troublesome neighbours, disruptive youths, vagrants and their squalor and so on (Taylor 1995, Girling *et al.* 2000), rather than around horrendous and sporadic crimes committed far away.

In the United States, zero tolerance policing became one way – there has also been the use of trespass and loitering laws (Davis 1992, Beckett 2005) – of using the power of the criminal justice system rather than social services to improve the quality of life of ordinary law-abiding citizens. Zero tolerance focussed *not* on prosecuting all crime but instead on 'low level infringements of the law, public drinking, jay walking and the activities of graffiti artists and squeegie merchants, on the grounds that these are the forms of behaviour that make citizens feel unsafe in public places' (McLaughlin 2001: 323). In Britain, New Labour's Crime and Disorder Act 1998 and Anti-Social Behaviour Act 2003 allowed for the prosecution of a whole range of 'incivilities' as well as minor crime. A hybrid measure which could be applied to any behaviour, the legislation provides for civil injunctions to be used in the first instance. Thereafter, any breaches of these orders are to be prosecuted through the criminal courts and can lead to a maximum of five years' imprisonment. Between 1998 and 2005 only around 5,000 orders were made. However, the number is not only increasing but the authorities have been actively encouraged to make more use of these measures by central government – indeed these have become performance indicators for the police and other local authority officials (*The Guardian* 2 September 2005: 2).

Such initiatives are exemplars of penal populism. The 1998 Act was described by the then Home Secretary as 'a triumph for democratic politics – in truth a victory for local communities over *detached metropolitan elites*.'[10] This is because, until the advent of measures such as these, it seemed to be the case that the interests of ordinary people, in relation to such immediate problems of social order, were neglected by or were in conflict with those of an inactive, uncaring local government bureaucracy. Even if its officials did try to intervene, they had little by way of sanction available to them. If the criminal law had to be relied on, then, as Tony Blair (quoted by Millie *et al*. 2005: 18) has explained, 'it is next to impossible for the police to prosecute without a protracted court process, bureaucracy and hassle, when conviction will only result in a minor sentence. Hence the new powers to take swift summary action.' In these respects, the anti-social behaviour legislation bypasses seemingly outmoded criminal justice processes. For example, the authorities can now proceed against those under the age of criminal responsibility by making their parents legally responsible for their actions. At the same time it recognizes what the existing law had not been able to do, since, in isolation, one minor offence or one incident of anti-social behaviour might indeed not amount to very much. However, under the new legislation, 'We can now address *the cumulative impact* of a range of incidents and behaviours which, individually, might seem relatively minor but become intolerable when endured on a daily basis' (Hansen *et al*. 2003: 84, my italics). As such, the legal principles and technicalities that the local state had relied on in the past as a justification for inaction have been bypassed. The new law provides for responses to the kind of behaviour – not necessarily criminal – that was likely to make every day life intolerable – thereby placing the interests of 'the people' above those of criminal justice officials.

But why should it be that 'even apparently minor acts' – as with the child kicking a football against a wall above – are able to make such an impact and provoke such a reaction against them? Comments made by a member of one local authority mediation service give a good indication: 'the sort of things that we deal with on a daily basis are noise and various other forms of nuisance – *anything where there can be any interaction really*: competition for shared facilities: driveways, boundaries, hedges' (House of Commons Home Affairs Committee 2005: 25, my italics). Human interaction has become as problematic as this because of what Christie (2004: 69–70) refers to as 'the extermination of primary relations' – the decline of viable geographical communities, a mobile but transient labour force, the breakdown of interpersonal dependencies and so on.

And, of course, it is likely to be on the sink estates and ghettos – those areas where primary relations are weakest – that incivilities or anti-social behaviour can seem the most acute and the most unsolvable by informal means. Without state intervention, there is unlikely to be any easy escape from such unending unpleasantness. Home Office Minister Hazel Blears thus stated in 2005 that:

> [H]aving nuisance neighbours may sound trivial to some, but the reality can be pure hell for the individuals and communities affected. In the worst cases, the anti-social behaviour of one or two families can hold whole streets to ransom, causing residents to live in fear of vandalism, abuse or harassment, day in, day out.
>
> (www.direct.gov.uk/output/page7115.asp)

I am not denying that there is a reality to the phenomenon of incivilities and anti-social behaviour: it is not simply that such behaviours have stayed the same while everything around them has changed (cf Squires and Stephens 2005). However, while Tony Blair has increasingly referred to 'lack of respect'[11] as being at the core of such conduct, in many modern societies, the necessary *social conditions* for respect – commitment, trust, tolerance, loyalty, stability – are dissolving: indeed, some of these qualities are now regarded as undesirable or outmoded contemporary values – they are seen only as impediments to personal success (Bauman 2004). As Richard Sennett (2005: 2) has written:

> [T]oday deference has lost its cultural value and perhaps rightly so. It doesn't suit a democratic age. But with the decline of deference has also gone the exchange . . . the phrase 'a culture of respect' should imply more than curbing offensive behaviour. People need to feel that they matter to others.

As we have seen, however, the new divisions in modern society do not easily generate such interdependencies and bonds. Without these necessary social conditions for respect and the transmission of a civic culture, then there will inevitably be regular displays of incivilities and regular displays of intolerance to them. In addition to the acute antagonisms that this interaction leads to on the sink estates, countless others take place across other levels of society. However carefully boundaries have been constructed to keep out the menace and unseemliness of the unwanted and undesirable, there is always the worry that these can be breached. Indeed, nowhere seems free from such possibilities, however hard one has worked to build these boundaries. Girling *et al.* (2000: 77–8) thus write of Prestbury, one of the wealthiest villages in England, where to buy is:

> [T]o purchase a pleasurable, excessive retreat, a 'safe haven' for oneself, one's family and one's children, an environment bracketed off from the troubles of the outside world. This is something that many of its residents have taken on hefty – often anxiety-inducing, success-dependent – financial commitments in order to enjoy. Hence the intensely felt feelings of disquiet, disappointment and anger that attach to locally occurring instances of crime and disorder.

Teenagers who had colonized the centre of the village and claimed this as their own (ibid.: 75) were largely responsible for this. Residents in such settings will understandably feel cheated on finding that even when they have been as successful in life as most of us can aspire to be ('this is a place for those who are climbing up, or who have prospered in or retired from the worlds of global finance, enterprise and the professions' [ibid.: 65]), order and security remain at risk.

In different settings, the visible presence of the homeless and other street people provides the potential for regular collisions between the two worlds of affluence and indulgence on the one hand and destitution and menace on the other. Prior to his zero tolerance policing in New York, Brattan (1997: 34) describes:

> [P]roceeding down Fifth Avenue, the mile of designer stores and famous buildings, unlicensed street peddlers and beggars are everywhere. Then down into the subway where everyday over two hundred thousand fare evaders jumped over or under the turnstiles while shakedown artists vandalised turnstiles and demanded that paying passengers hand over their tickets to them . . . Every platform seemed to have a cardboard city where the homeless had taken up residence . . . The city had lost control.

Such sights do more than simply tarnish the image that a

modern city likes to project for itself – safe, affluent and free from such impurities; in addition, they are indicators of a society that seems to have broken down, sights that would not be possible in a society that was functioning as it should be.[12]

As such, the anti-social behaviour legislation and corresponding initiatives in the United States and other jurisdictions speak to these anxieties and represent assurances that the city, or local community, or the state has 'taken back control', is again capable of reasserting its authority: fixed penalties, parenting orders, acceptable behaviour contracts, naming and shaming strategies and so on, many of which are also highly publicized sanctions, provide clearly understandable and visible affirmations of this. At the same time, the anti-social behaviour legislation and its counterparts elsewhere attempt to cement the relationship between populist governments and the people, at the expense of the elitist critics of these measures, those 'people whose comfortable notions of human behaviour [are] matched only by their comfortable distance from its worst excesses' (Home Secretary Jack Straw quoted by Ryan 2004: 17).

Overall, crime control policy influenced by penal populism no longer fits the bifurcated approach that preceded it. It is more likely to be contingent, opportunistic and *ad hoc* than logical and consistent. Its general intent is to provide protection against unwanted or undesirable others. Depending on the strength of penal populism in a given jurisdiction, levels of protection can extend from the predations of the most monstrous of sex offenders to the child kicking a football against a wall. At the same time, it is prepared to break down the barriers that the criminal justice establishment had placed around the previous limits of punishment and control to provide this protection.

5

COMPETING AND COMPLEMENTARY INFLUENCES ON PENAL STRATEGY AND THOUGHT

Whatever presence it gains in a given jurisdiction, penal populism does not exist in isolation from a range of other, sometimes competing, sometimes complimentary influences on penal strategy and thought. Failure to acknowledge this has been a regular shortcoming of scholarship in this area, as Matthews (2005) reminds us. Indeed, the almost exclusive focus on penal populism, at the expense of any consideration of these other influences, may lead to the production of what O'Malley (2000) has referred to as 'criminologies of catastrophe', whereby the realities of penal populism would be exaggerated and distorted. As Brown (2005: 36) puts the matter, 'undue weight may be given to the exceptional and the excessive, while tendencies which seem to indicate that the opposite is happening may be played down or overlooked.'

To avoid doing so, this chapter considers the relationship between penal populism and these other influences. In these respects, it would seem particularly apposite to return to Bottoms (1995) as a starting point. There, 'populist punitiveness' was reviewed in conjunction with the three other 'main movements of thought that [then] seemed to underpin much of modern sentencing change in different countries' (ibid.: 18) – these being: just deserts/human rights; managerialism and invocations of 'community'. However, in now providing an updated exposition of these influences, three modifications have been made to Bottoms' original matrix. First, as might be expected of such a dynamic arena, it has not been the case that this has remained unchanged. The other three influences alongside populist punitiveness/penal populism have themselves undergone some reconfiguration; and they have also been joined by two more in the intervening period: *restorative and reparative penalties*, and *incapacitatory, restrictive and disqualificatory penalties*. Second, of his original four 'movements of thought', it seemed to Bottoms (1995: 48, my italics) that:

> [T]here are reasonable grounds for believing that most criminal-justice systems will contain some features reflecting the themes of just deserts/human rights, managerialism and community; *but that is not necessarily the case as regards populist punitiveness, that factor being potentially more closely tied to short-term political considerations.*

A decade or so later, penal populism has become one of the most significant and recognized influences on penal development, rather than being the one with the most unpromising future. This has occurred at the expense of some of the competing influences on strategy and thought, but has also occurred with the facilitation of others. Penological influences are not mutually exclusive – this is the third qualification: developments in one may make possible growth in another. Penal thought and strategies are marked by fluidity and overlap rather than rigid compartmentalization.

It should also be understood that this chapter is written not by way of criticism of Bottoms' (1995) important and much cited contribution to penological knowledge, but in recognition that a good part of the argument set out there has since simply been overtaken by events. Bottoms himself argued that the disembedding processes of modern society were already impacting on penal thought. From the examination of these forces that has been undertaken in this book, it would seem that their effects have since accelerated. Overall, these, rather than 'short-term political considerations', are the pre-conditions for penal populism. Since the early 1990s, public concerns about insecurity, the decline of authority and fear of crime have been made manifest in monsters previously unknown to modern society – predators, stalkers, neighbours from hell and so on. It is their presence – somewhere out there, even if we are not exactly sure where – which seems to be emblematic of a society where stability and security has broken down and which has led to populist demands for tougher punishments as a way of restoring these pillars of support on which it can rest.

However, this does not then mean that there are no limits to the growth of penal populism once it takes root in a particular jurisdiction. Each one is likely to have specific in-built defences to curb its progress. We are also beginning to see signs that the resources it demands for its programme of punishment cannot be supplied indefinitely: in other words, there are natural limits to how far a populist penal programme can be pursued.

JUST DESERTS / HUMAN RIGHTS

Bottoms (1995: 22) claimed that 'in many jurisdictions, ranging from Sweden to the United Kingdom to the

United States, [just deserts] influence has been substantial.'
He was undoubtedly correct at the time and since then there
is no doubt that just deserts has enjoyed continuing influence, particularly, for example, in the writing of Scandinavian penal codes, with low mandatory minimum sentences
(von Hirsch 1993, Tham 1995). Equally, in the United
States, Minnesota, a state which seems to have the most
highly developed sentencing grid for the purposes of implementing the just deserts philosophy, and which limits
judicial discretion within narrow maximum and minimum
bands (von Hirsch *et al*. 1987), has one of the lowest state
levels of imprisonment in that country (although at 226 per
100,000 of population this still puts it way ahead of all other
OECD countries). In contrast, the English Criminal Justice
Act 1991 which had been strongly influenced by this philosophy quickly became politically unacceptable and the principles of proportionality that were ensconced within it were
largely abandoned. Instead, the emphasis has since been on
punishment fitting the criminal rather than the crime. Those
elements of liberal individualism which had informed the
just deserts philosophy now seem to have given way to a
much more intolerant punitiveness.

Such developments do not mean, of course, that the
principle of just deserts (and its much more longstanding
philosophical predecessor 'retribution') has altogether faded
from the sentencing arena. Principles of consistency and proportionality are obviously still used to justify sentencing on
an everyday basis in England, even if this philosophy has
become significantly less influential *on general policy development*. Elsewhere, the New Zealand Sentencing Act 2002
emphasized the importance of proportionality in punishment, with the Minister of Justice claiming that the new
law would 'establish a fair, firm and rational sentencing
framework that delivers clarity and consistency' (quoted by
Roberts 2003: 257), all of which (with the exception of the

ambiguous word 'firm'), would seem to fit comfortably within the just deserts paradigm. However, the same legislation has also contributed to that country's escalating prison levels – the rate of imprisonment increased from 110 per 100,000 of population in 1990 to 145 in 2003, then to 189 in 2006 – by providing for longer prison terms, particularly for sexual and violent offenders, and by effectively 'normalizing' indefinite detention. Furthermore, the legislation was passed amidst a general exhortation that judges should use longer prison sentences, and be much more ready to make use of maximum sentences (see p. 15), rather than the proportionate or even parsimonious punishments that would be consistent with just deserts.

If this would seem to confirm the way in which we can expect to find a range of competing and conflicting influences on penal thought and policy development at any given time, rather than the supreme dominance of any one of them, it would also seem to point to the way in which just deserts, without a fairly rigid sentencing grid or penal code that then ties it firmly to low levels of penal magnitude, is likely to become a hostage to political fortune, as even its staunchest proponents acknowledge (von Hirsch and Ashworth 1998). It is a floating concept – what constitutes proportionate punishment is open to all kinds of interpretations and variations – which can be inflated and expanded to suit populist demands. As we have seen, this is what happened in the United States during the 1980s, and this is what has happened in New Zealand in the first decade of this century. Sentence lengths can easily be raised to suit changing political and cultural understandings of what constitutes proportionality.

By the same token, just deserts' *commonsensical* associations with retribution convey a sense that something akin to 'revenge' should influence sentencing, again encouraging the kind of unforgiving mood associated with penal populism, while simultaneously reducing any ameliorative tendencies in sentencing practices (although ironically, of course, its Kantian philosophical origins specify that retribution is intended to be an essentially *limiting* influence on punishment).[1] In these respects, while most jurisdictions will still contain elements of just deserts thinking, although at a declining level in some, the philosophy may also serve as a conduit for emotive populist sentiments rather than limiting the space for them.

That said, there is no doubt that there has at the same time been a growing emphasis on the protection of the *human rights* of accused and prisoners – although it could also be argued that this has been exponential to the rate in which these have been put at risk by the successes and excesses of populism over the same period: prison overcrowding and the retrenchment of more liberal and relaxed conditions put in place in most of the anglophone countries in the late 1980s and early 1990s as a way of 'relegitimating' the prison after decades of crisis (Sparks 1994); or the adaptation of particularly harsh prison regimes by the prison authorities which get caught up in the new mood of punitiveness. Thus, in the United States, under the ominous banner 'Back to Basics in Georgia's Prisons' the Georgia Department of Corrections Annual Report (1996: 13) proudly boasts that it is 'one of the most responsive states' to enact 'tough on crime legislation.'

As a signifier of the way in which 'the prisoner is now regarded, to a much greater extent than thirty or forty years ago, as a person with rights', Bottoms (1995: 23) was able to refer to the British case of Doody[2] which then seemed to point towards a more open approach to giving prisoners information about administrative decisions affecting their release dates. A little more than a decade later, Justice Michael Kirby's (dissenting) judgment in the Australian case of Muir v The Queen ([2004] HCA 21, 25) well captures the spirit in which the protection of such rights may now be pursued in law:

> Prisoners are human beings. In most cases, they are also cit-
> izens of this country, 'subjects of the Queen' . . . They should,
> so far as the law can allow, ordinarily have the same rights as all
> other persons before this Court. They have lost their liberty
> whilst they are in prison. However, so far as I am concerned,
> they have not lost their human dignity or their right to equality
> before the law.

Indeed, the United Nations has adopted Standard Minimum Rules for the Treatment of Prisoners. These are also covered in the European Convention on Human Rights and many countries now have their own Human Rights Act, which extends to prisoners. The protection of prisoners' rights is included in the United Nations International Covenant on Economic, Social and Cultural Rights and a similar Covenant on Civil and Political Rights.

At the same time, the globalizing influences which have weakened local state autonomy and have given encouragement to penal populism, have also provided new venues to seek justice when remedies are exhausted in local jurisdictions – the European Court of Human Rights, for example. Furthermore, the growing interest in human rights has led to the proliferation of local and international bodies designed to protect them. In the 1970s Amnesty International was probably the only such organization working in this area. There are now numerous others, local and international, such as Penal Reform International, Human Rights Watch, the American Civil Liberties Union and The Prison Reform Trust.

Be this as it may, the British courts have since been reluctant to extend the principles established in Doody.[3] One reason for this may relate to changes to the way in which human rights issues have been addressed by governments in the intervening period. It seemed to Bottoms that these concerns had grown in response to the excessive state power which had been incorporated in the treatment and rehabilitation model that had been the predominant influence on penology in the post-war period (at least up to the 1970s): one of the ways to protect the rights of the individual prisoner against such encroachments had been to limit the use of the indeterminate prison sentence. Now, however, the exercise of excessive power over the individual prisoner or defendant by the state is regularly justified on behalf of 'community interests'. While this has been most clearly and publicly debated in relation to the introduction of new terrorist legislation, community interests in more mundane criminal justice contexts have been allowed to outweigh the rights of individual criminals in jurisdictions where penal populism has had a strong impact: in relation to rights of privacy against community notification procedures, for example; rights of protection under the double jeopardy rule against sexual predator laws; and rights to proportionate and finite punishment against the growing recourse to indeterminate sentences of imprisonment.[4]

This is not to say, of course, that the courts will no longer protect often longstanding rights of accused or prisoners now put at risk in such ways. However, in the existing penal climate, particularly in those societies where penal populism had has a marked impact, victory in the courts may prove to be of a pyrrhic nature. The very assertion that prisoners have human rights may be regarded by those outside of the liberal legal establishment which proclaims them as an affront which only generates further populist excesses. In New Zealand, the High Court and then the Court of Appeal found that the confinement of six complainant prisoners in a 'Behaviour Management Regime' – in effect, in conditions similar to those in an American supermax prison (King 1999) – had no lawful authority and was in breach of the New Zealand Bill of Rights Act (Taunoa v Attorney General [2004] 7 HRNZ 379). Although it was held that this did not amount to torture, nonetheless, 'the Corrections [Department] failed to treat prisoners on the Behaviour Management Regime with humanity and failed to treat them with the inherent dignity due every person' (ibid., para 277).

The case then generated outrage from the general public and from politicians: outrage not that prisoners' rights could be so flagrantly violated and abused, but that these prisoners could actually receive (modest) damages for the ill-treatment and abuse they had experienced. This had lasted, in the case of one of them, for three years. In response, the Labour government rushed through the Prisoners and Victims Claims Act 2005. The legislation, which applies to cases already before the courts pending final determination, and thus has a retrospective element, allows victims of crime and their families to sue ex-prisoners for financial compensation for up to six years after their release, should they come by any windfall: for example, a winning lottery ticket, or even the assets built up by pursuing a successful career after prison, *or the receipt of damages awarded in cases such as the above*: 'the Bill restricts as much as possible the circumstances that might give rise to compulsory payments to inmates. Where payments are made, it maximises the prospect that victims will be the beneficiaries, and I make no apologies for that', explained the Justice Minster (New Zealand Government 2004).

Such developments would seem to suggest that there has been something of a retreat by governments from further expansions of the human rights of prisoners – as might be expected in societies where there is now such a division between 'ordinary people' and all those 'others' thought to encroach on the former's rights to security and order. As Michael Howard, leader of the British Conservative Party explained in 2004: 'there is now a palpable sense of outrage that so called human rights have tipped the balance of justice in favour of the criminal and wrong-doer, rather than the victim and the law-abider.'[5] The state's duty is now to protect and uphold the rights of the law abiding citizen, with the forfeiture, if necessary, of the rights of those who put this at risk. Furthermore, as far as some politicians are concerned, if such forfeiture is in breach of codes and covenants meant to be guaranteed by supra-national organizations such as the United Nations, then so much the better. By being prepared to either dismiss the rights of accused or prisoners that such bodies now try to guarantee, or by not being prepared to grant them any further extensions, not only are they asserting the rights and interests of ordinary people over these 'others', but at the same time they are asserting national sovereignty over the interdictions of far-distant unelected officials: which seems likely to only increase the contestation of human rights issues and strengthen the appeal of populism.[6]

MANAGERIALISM

This concept refers to those methods employed – as in other public sector areas such as transport, education and health – to make the criminal justice system as a whole more cost-effective, efficient and publicly accountable. To this effect, it necessitates an emphasis on inter-agency co-operation, to ensure that all parts of the system are functioning as one; the development of an overall strategic plan, which all parts of the system are meant to work towards; the development of 'mission statements', to guide the direction of each part; the development of key performance indicators to assess their effectiveness; and the monitoring of aggregate information about the system to determine its overall effectivity (see, on these points, Bottoms 1995: 25).

This 'systemic' managerialism (ibid.) also involves the publication of annual reports, replete with pictograms and diagrams, technical assessments and efficiency gauges – but which actually *say* very little at all. There is no longer any place in these reports for the moralistic and opinionative language of the British Prison Commissioners which was so characteristic of their report writing from the late nineteenth century to the early 1960s. Their views were regularly set out on how their particular 'system' should function, usually quite independently of any consideration for the broader system of which it was a part; indeed, rather than this, it was as if they 'owned' their system and overtures from others that touched on it were thought to be unnecessary and unwelcome.[7] The Report of the Prison Commissioners (1954: 1), for example, magisterially observes that 'we have noted with regret that public comment on the state of discipline in prisons has sometimes tended to give the impression that . . . there has been a deterioration giving ground for anxiety. This is not the case.' Now, however, the compliant managerialist language of throughputs and outputs, of efficiencies gained and targets achieved, give these organizations political neutrality: there is no attempt to address issues of which particular goals have been set and why. Managerialism provides no barrier to populism; instead, it simply provides a mechanism which allows criminal justice organizations to be carried along in its wake, as it redefines their tasks.

Nonetheless, it might still be thought that the use of actuarial decision-making – another aspect of managerialism – in the determination of decisions regarding parole applicants might be an effective rebuff to populism. Their 'risk to the community' which is now probably the most important parole criterion in most jurisdictions, is thereby 'scientifically' assessed, rather than swayed by commonsense public sentiment. However, the very presence of actuarialism may actually help to legitimate other bi-products and ancillaries of penal populism – the resurrection of dangerousness, indeterminate sentences and selective incapacitation. It allows bureaucratic organizations to avoid the moral consequences of their policies by relying on statistical computations rather than human judgements. As Bottoms (1995: 33) himself acknowledged, under such circumstances 'it may become difficult to counterpoise the traditional language of, for example, "justice" against the aggregative and instrumental assumptions of an actuarial approach.'

Bottoms (1995: 31) then drew attention to a third feature of managerialism – 'consumerism', whereby managers 'tend to become increasingly interested in the views of those to whom services are delivered, to test whether, in their view, the services are being delivered satisfactorily.' Again, with accelerating tendencies towards consumerism and market-ization taking place right across modern societies, there is no reason to expect criminal justice systems to be immune from such developments. However, unlike other sectors, it is clearly not the case that the views of *all* consumers of crimi-nal justice are being taken note of: indeed, outside the restorative justice sector (see p. 139), it seems that it is almost overwhelmingly the views of victims that are solicited, par-ticularly in the United States (Rock 2004), in what repre-sents a marked reversal of interests in the administration of justice. In much of post-war penal policy development, it had been the views of offenders which had been sought. Indeed, Leslie Wilkins stated that, in the 1950s, 'there was really a strong fear of victims. Victims were put in their place in court too . . . any organization of victims was going to be seen as potential vigilantism' (quoted by Rock 1990: 62).

As we have since seen, however, 'if victims were once the forgotten, hidden casualties of criminal behaviour, they have now returned with a vengeance, brought back into full public view by politicians and media executives' (Garland 2001: 143): in contrast to the almost complete silence that now envelops their offenders – as if their actions have said enough of their wickedness. Tony Blair (quoted by Solomon 2004: 6) has thus insisted that:

> The law-abiding citizen must be at the heart of our criminal justice system. For too long it was far from the case ... The system seemed to only think about the rights of the accused. The interests of victims appeared to be an afterthought, if considered at all.

To this end, in many jurisdictions, victims now play an important role in the adjudication of penalties and in the determination of parole for those who have offended against them. Their impact statements help to change the balance of the scales of justice – and are written by probation officers, which is another indication of this changing balance: contemporaneously, their report-writing for offenders has become much more of a pro-forma routine with less opportunity to act as offender advocate.

Furthermore, populist politicians and law and order groups also speak regularly on behalf of victims (with or without their permission), usually in terms of their perceived dissatisfaction with the existing criminal justice system and the criminal justice establishment ('on behalf of all New Zealanders, I am trying to exact justice for the victims of crime, something that politicians seem incapable of doing or are loathe to instigate', explained Norm Withers when campaigning for his referendum [*The Dominion* 12 May 1999: 2]). As such, the 'ownership' of criminal victimization has changed. It had previously belonged to a variety of women's groups in the 1980s and early 1990s. They had campaigned around issues of violence and sexual assault and had been influential on public responses to and investigations of these crimes, which they understood as the product of patriarchal power. However, as crime victimization began to receive more general attention, the concerns it generated came to be subsumed into a more general popular movement, leading to a significant shift in understandings of its causes and solutions. Increasingly, crime would be articulated by victims' – or potential victims' – representatives as the product of wicked or irresponsible 'others', needing to be addressed by the populist imperative of longer prison sentences rather than any feminist-influenced restructuring of gender relations.

COMMUNITY

Bottoms (1995: 34) suggested that this vague concept referred to three developments then taking place across contemporary penal systems: (i) community penalties and diversion; (ii) justice in and for local communities and groups; (iii) the devolution of criminal justice decision making to local communities. Since then, however, changes in the terms of penal debate have led to a significant reconfiguration of this term. The last of these three sub-categories pointed the way to what is now known as restorative justice. As this has since become a major 'movement of thought' in its own right, it is considered in more detail in the following section. In addition, though, 'community' seems to have taken on an extra meaning since 1995. It can be used to invoke new penal sanctions – usually punitive, restrictive and intrusive – against those who prey on a community's inhabitants and corrode its values. 'Community' in this sense has lost the implicit stability and capacity for self-regulation that it was previously assumed to have and which such measures are meant to protect and restore. Tony Blair (2005: 1) thus writes that, by 1997 when New Labour assumed office:

> [C]ommunities were more fractured, sometimes as a result of desirable objectives like social mobility or diversity, sometimes as the consequences of mass unemployment and failed economic policies. Civil institutions such as the church declined in importance. At the start of the twentieth century, communities

shared a strong moral code. By the end of the century, this was no longer true.

It is this new understanding of 'community' which may partly explain the declining emphasis given to community penalties, the first of Bottoms' sub-categories, designed to act as alternatives to custody that were characteristic of the 1980s, even the early 1990s policy development: as if communities have become too fragmented and unreliable to be able to sustain the management of offenders within them. Equally, as politicians have become more involved in discussions of penal affairs, usually with a view to protecting local communities from criminals, this has meant that they are inclined to express increasing scepticism of such penalties while reaffirming the necessity of prison. At the same time, it would also seem that public understandings of punishment are defined by the idea of prison – there is little knowledge of community punishments, other than suspicions that they might not amount to very much (see Hough and Roberts 1998; Dickey and Smith 1998; Roberts 2002).

As a result, it is not surprising to find that in countries such as New Zealand and England, where these political and public discourses have become so predominant since the mid 1990s, the use of community penalties (including those involving work and supervision) has declined while custodial sentences have increased.[8] It is also surely significant that in both these jurisdictions home detention and electronic monitoring of offenders, originally envisaged as an alternative to custody sentence, now operate as a form of early release from prison in conjunction with parole. In contrast, in Sweden, a country where penal populism has a presence (Tham 2001) but where it still does not seem to have generated the same degree of penal restructuring as in the above two countries, this provision seems to have had genuine success in being used as an alternative sanction to imprisonment (see Cavadino and Dignan 2005: 158). More generally, though, where penal populism has gained the greatest momentum, it seems that the possibilities for community punishments as a response to crime recedes, while the use of prison is increasingly normalized.

As regards the second 'community' sub-category, then, with the continuing fragmentation of social class, there have been increasingly more local communities and groups contesting state imposed versions of justice, claiming legitimacy instead for their own definitions of what this should be. However, groups such as these stand in direct opposition to penal populism and its constituency of 'normal', ordinary people who are assumed to be law-abiding and who are likely to take the view that 'justice' is indivisible: for them, it can only mean the protection of the innocent and the punishment of the guilty. We may then find that this very contestation of 'justice' gives encouragement to penal populism rather than limits its possibilities. Populism seems able to recognize that the very plethora of rights groups now in existence is itself a signifier of the fractured and dissolving nature of local communities, while holding out ways of returning them to their previous homogeneity and solidity, where everyone had the same understanding of what 'justice' was.

RESTORATIVE AND REPARATIVE PENALTIES

There has been a phenomenal growth in the restorative justice movement across much of Western society since the mid 1990s (Mika and Zehr 2003). From the victim and offender mediation schemes and family group conferences then in existence:

> Restorative justice is [now] used not only in adult and juvenile criminal matters, but also in a range of civil matters, including

> family welfare and child protection, and disputes in schools and workplace settings. Increasingly, one finds the term associated with the resolution of broader political conflicts such as the reconstruction of post-apartheid South Africa, post-genocide Rwanda, and post-sectarian Northern Ireland.
>
> (Daly 2002: 57)

Local communities have indeed been empowered to put their own stamp on criminal justice decision-making, whether this be in the form of Canadian sentencing circles, family group conferences as in New Zealand, English juvenile offender panels and so on.

Furthermore, because of its emphasis on reintegrating offenders (Braithwaite 1989) rather than excluding them – which is the certain consequence of populist driven policy – restorative justice clearly does provide the opportunity for a fundamentally non-stigmatic approach to the sanctioning of crime and the resolution of social conflict. However, in most jurisdictions it is likely – because it is more bureaucratically convenient as much as for any other reason – that it will simply be grafted onto existing criminal justice and penal processes, rather than bringing about the more fundamental justice paradigm shift that it initially signalled (Morris and Maxwell 1993). Even so, it may still have the capacity to liberalize and humanize those areas that it touches, bringing about a broader transformation of existing criminal justice processes by means of such infiltration (Braithwaite and Parker 1999). Thus, in England, restorative justice is used to strengthen pre-court cautioning processes and make them more efficient. In addition, juvenile offender panels preside over youth justice processes which make victims and offenders more central to the proceedings: 'the 'conflict' is to be 'resolved, or the 'harm' is to be 'repaired' by offender reparation and apology. As Crawford and Newburn (2002: 479) write:

> There are several important 'restorative' and 'reintegrative' aspects to the[se] new provisions. [The panels] adopt a conference-type approach to decision making that is intended to be both inclusive and party-centred . . . as such, they mark a significant shift away from a court-based judicial model in which the parties are represented rather than speak for themselves.

Nonetheless, restorative justice has become almost as vague a term as 'community' itself, with the attendant possibility that it might simply become one element of a stronger, coercive body designed to provide more efficient penal control (ibid.). On this matter, Rock (2004: 288) notes that in the United States the term has been used to include 'even sex offender notification laws, and the rights of relatives of murder victims to be present at executions were deemed restorative by some.' In New Zealand, the Justice Minister declared that the Prisoners and Victims Claims Act was an example of restorative justice: that is, offenders would be made to recompense their victims, although the nature of the compensation goes far beyond anything envisaged in idealist prescriptions of restorative justice. In effect, under this legislation, it can mean that any attempt by ex-offenders to better and improve their living standards can be forfeit to those they have offended against, long after their prison sentence has been served. Rather than facilitating the reintegration of offenders, the concept of restorative justice is used here to justify their continued penalization and the imposition of secondary punishments. Merely going to prison is no longer punishment enough: as the Justice Minister explained, 'it costs us $NZ50,000 a year to keep someone in prison . . . that is a cost to society, not the repayment of a debt . . . you don't repay your debt to the victim by being in prison' (*The Dominion Post* 8 January 2005: E3).

What this would suggest is that, once the term 'restorative justice' is co-opted into official discourse, it can lose both its oppositional focus and its specificity, and is effectively 'captured': it becomes a catchall phrase to be used for whatever purposes a government wants, usually far removed from its original purposes of assisting victims in healing and reintegrating offenders. The overall result may thus be that, rather than colonizing from within, restorative justice itself becomes that which is colonized.

Furthermore, the very language in which restorative justice is articulated, even if in tune with the sensibilities of the liberal establishment which increasingly presides over its development,[9] seems likely to alienate public support rather than attract it, to drive the public towards penal populism rather than away from it. The emphasis on 'harms' and 'conflicts', rather than crimes; on 'putting things right' rather than punishing, seems at best likely to provoke distrust and suspicion, if not full-scale alarm, which may help to explain the dramatically low attendance of victims at 'restorative sessions' in Britain (see Newburn *et al.* 2002, Hoyle 2002). Again, the way in which restorative justice (at least for some significant constituencies within it) seems to be framed around notions of victims as latter-day Jesus Christ figures, ultimately understanding, empathizing with and forgiving those who have 'wronged' them (that is, have committed crimes against them) is at odds with that more fundamentalist and more recognizably understandable Old-Testament victim that penal populism has conjured, addresses and speaks for: one who is unforgiving, implacable and demands not apologies and piecemeal reparation but protection and punishment. Thus Norm Withers, when campaigning for his New Zealand referendum, claimed that 'he had spoken to hundreds of victims of serious violence and only one had agreed with the [restorative justice family group] conference idea. The others did not want to see their attackers again' (*The Press* 28 December 1998: 2).

This is not to recognize, of course, the potential that restorative justice clearly does possess to challenge the concepts and strategies of penal populism. While these may be raising prison levels at one end of the penal spectrum, in other areas restorative justice strategies are making important inroads in transforming both formal and informal local justice practices, avoiding both the unresponsive bureaucratic detachment associated with the former and the repressive brutality that can emerge from the latter. McEvoy and Mika (2002: 556) have demonstrated these possibilities in relation to Northern Ireland where restorative justice has mitigated against the punishment violence of sectarian authorities. Equally, Clifford Shearing (2001) has shown with regard to South Africa that it is possible to develop models of interaction between the state and its poorest communities which maximize people's ability to take control over the direction of their own lives without the original programmes then being swallowed by state infrastructure.

Whether restorative justice will be able to construct such alternative justice modalities or be engulfed and overwhelmed by populist-inspired penal developments *in mainstream modern society* remains to be seen. In both the above examples, it flourishes where the state either has no legitimacy, or where a new state formation is being constructed. In most Western countries, penal populism, not restorative justice, has gained where it seems it can *restore state authority*, not replace it with something new and unfamiliar: for many, the world is already troubling enough, without these attempts by restorative justice proponents to take them into more unexplored territories.

INCAPACITATORY, RESTRICTIVE AND DISQUALIFICATORY PENALTIES

As restorative justice has gathered momentum, so too have increasingly potent forces at the other end of the penal spectrum which have sought to exclude, restrict or disqualify some groups of offenders on a more or less permanent basis: three strikes laws and community notification and protection legislation provide clear examples of this trend. At the same time, penal populism reinvigorates provisions already in existence, such as preventive detention, designed to achieve similar results. Ethical barriers which had previously been placed in the way of such strategies can now be overridden because of the imperative of placing community interests and well-being over and above those of individual law breakers. Meanwhile, for those whose incapacitation is not permanent and who are eventually released, or for many of those who are dealt with by way of community penalties, any subsequent attempts to rebuild their lives may be fraught with interference, restriction and prohibitions about where they can go and with whom they can associate.[10] Indeed, as the authority of the state declines, local communities, often egged on by populist politicians may themselves expel unwanted ex-prisoners.[11]

Bottoms (1995: 40–1) claimed that where penal populism was particularly influential, the incapacitatory strategies it encouraged would become one aspect of an exaggerated bifurcation of crime control policy. The logic is clear enough. 'Behind the scenes' policy makers shuffle their resources away from provisions for non-serious offenders and instead use them to provide additional measures to control the serious, in an attempt to convince the public that their concerns are being met, while avoiding putting extra burdens on public expenditure to do so. To a certain extent, this has happened. While the New Zealand Sentencing Act (2002) prescribed longer sentences for 'serious offenders', the Parole Act (2002), which received far less public and political scrutiny, eased parole criteria for those serving shorter sentences.

However, it can also be the case that the stronger penal populism becomes, then the less likely we will find the bifurcated crime control policy that Bottoms suggested would eventuate. Penal populism has nothing to gain from attempts to 'define deviance down' at the less serious end of the offending spectrum – to do so might only have the effect of throwing water on the fires it has started. Instead, it can present an implacable and resolute face against various categories of major and minor criminals. British Home Secretary Jack Straw, for example, claimed in 1997:

> Today's young offenders can too easily become tomorrow's hardened criminals. For too long we have assumed they will grow out of their offending behaviour if left to themselves . . . an excuse culture has developed within the youth justice system . . . it excuses itself for its inefficiency and too often excuses young offenders who come before it, allowing them to go on wasting their own and wreck other people's lives.
>
> (quoted by Muncie 1999: 148)

As we have seen, in Britain and the United States especially (but elsewhere as well)[12] quality of life offending is prosecuted as a matter of urgency, rather than ignored, and restrictions are placed on indigent and surplus populations, effectively driving them out of areas of affluence and enterprise where they have no legitimate presence.

In addition, the concept of redemption – of having paid for one's crime with the court-imposed penalty but then being free to start life over again – has become another casualty of penal populism. In some jurisdictions there is a tendency to impose *ex post facto disqualificatory* penalties in addition to court-imposed sanctions. Hence the prohibition of persons convicted of serious violence and sexual offending (that is, an offence of this nature which is punishable by seven years imprisonment) from driving taxis, buses or trains in New Zealand under the provisions of the Land Transport Act 2005. The retrospective legislation was passed in the aftermath of a small number of well-publicized cases involving sexual assaults committed by taxi drivers.[13] Its subsequent effect has been to strip about 100 drivers, many of whom have had otherwise unblemished records for decades, of their livelihood on the basis of convictions that would now be considered trivial – and in spite of the advice of transport officials that the proposals would lead to exactly these consequences.[14] As one member of the Select Committee which formulated the legislation explained:

> We did ask for advice on prohibiting people from being passenger service drivers based on their having obtained very serious sexual or other violent convictions in the past. Once we had received that advice, we were [still] unanimous in our recommendation to alter the Bill to include prior convictions. We made the point that this is not only about passenger safety – it is about public confidence in the passenger service industry. Everyone is entitled to know that he or she is not getting into a taxi whose driver is a murderer or rapist. Nothing will change that.
>
> ([New Zealand] Hansard 10 May 2005, 20434)

IN-BUILT DEFENCES AGAINST PENAL POPULISM

Overall, it would seem that penal populism has become a significantly stronger force than was envisaged in 1995. Other influences have declined in significance; there are some which clearly stand in opposition to it, while still others have facilitated its rise or are directly linked to it. Having said this, then it is also clear that penal systems are likely to have their own in-built defences which put limits on how far its influence can be extended. This is because such institutions are 'deep structures', the product of incremental growth and successive layers of development built on top of each other over at least two centuries, containing the product and amalgamation of a mass of competing political, philosophical and bureaucratic interests. They are made up of so many different parts that, although they are meant to operate as a 'system', there are huge differences in the outlook and perspectives of individual segments of the whole and individual members of each segment. For example, as Freiberg (2000) has illustrated, judges are often likely to subvert the intent of what they consider to be excessively punitive legislation, particularly in relation to the use of indeterminate prison sentences. The powerfully symbolic boot camps (see p. 106) were quickly dropped when introduced outside the United States because of their ineffectiveness (in terms of reconviction rates) and their costs.

Furthermore, when members of the criminal justice establishment act in unison, they can still present a formidable and sometimes insurmountable barrier for populism to climb. In parts of the anglophone world, as a result of politicians continuing to resist populist flirtations with attempts to reinstate the death penalty, and now backed up by a range of supra-national organizations such as the EU and their covenants against it, popular support for this sanction is dwindling away. Indeed, the way in which punishments to the human body are simply disappearing as a cultural possibility in modern society (outside the United States) is a remarkable and largely unheralded testament to the achievements of principled politicians and their advisers in the criminal justice establishment. In other respects, and as a more bathetic example, in Britain, while Tony Martin became a populist hero, 'a victim who hit back', as William Hague, Leader of the Conservative party described him

(Rock 2004: 343), this kind of romanticization was widely criticized by the Bar's Public Relations Committee, the Secretary of the Law Society's Criminal Law Committee, the Association of Chief Police Officers and members of the judiciary. The Chairman of the Parole Board described Martin as 'a very dangerous man' (ibid.: 304). Support for Martin was severely criticized by Britain's broadsheet newspapers, with *The Times* (27 April 2000: 8) stating that Mr Hague's approach 'is likely to lead to prompt accusations that he is encouraging people to take the law into their hands.' In effect, this united front showed that the establishment was still sufficiently powerful enough to draw a line that populist forces on this occasion would not be allowed to cross (Rock 2004: 345).

Similarly in relation to the demands for Sarah's Law, led principally by the *News of the World*. Again, all the main criminal justice organizations, as well as government representatives were united in opposition: community notification should mean, for them, the sharing of information amongst communities of professionals – it should not be open to public access as in America: which, notwithstanding some gestures that *were made* towards allowing the public to become involved in drawing up local risk assessment guidelines (see p. 73), is the position that has been maintained in Britain. This case also demonstrated a further in-built defence against populism. After several weeks, the public protests ran out of steam. Law and order pressure groups tend to be fragile organizations: once they have made some impact, even if not the full impact they hoped for, they can then very easily dissipate.[15] Perhaps, in addition, the extent of the vigilantism that had taken place had a sobering effect on those this case had agitated. What most people who are sympathetic to populism want is *a reassertion of state authority*, rather than any further weakening of this.

In contrast to such loosely held together populist organizations, law societies, judiciaries, parole boards and the like have the advantage of a permanent presence in the criminal justice arena. For the most part, their size, lineage and institutional memory will make it very difficult for one set of ideas to fully colonize them, particularly when these come from the extra-establishment forces of penal populism. Thus in relation to the Australian state of New South Wales, Brown (2005: 36, my italics) writes of 'the resilience [of] a battered and reconfigured penal welfarism' which had dominated penal development in most modern societies for much of the nineteenth and twentieth centuries, despite the presence of populist strains from the late 1980s:

> It is probably true that at a more general level there is a trend of decreasing interest in and sympathy for prisoners, a hardened public sensibility against offenders and a lack of concern over the treatment of prisoners, although this is more evident in relation to selective notorious offenders, offences of violence and is far more ambiguous in relation to juveniles and less serious offenders ... *[however] such changes in cultural sensibilities have not necessarily been translated on the ground into more punitive practices, at least in any uniform way.*

In effect, in this jurisdiction, penal populism seems to have been experienced more at the level of rhetoric than substance.

More generally, populism remains one force amongst a range of others influencing penal development – a significantly more potent force than in the mid 1990s, but one with unpredictable potential *because local circumstances and contingencies are so important to it*; these can produce the effects that we have seen in California and New Zealand, for example, but are unlikely to replicate these elsewhere.[16] It does not work to one central blueprint. It may well be that penal populism is little more than rhetoric in some jurisdictions. Elsewhere, though, it develops into a remarkably pernicious force which increases all the pains of punishment on those criminals who receive the extra measures it is able to generate for them; and all the pains of victimization on those victims whose misfortunes it exploits and manipulates. And for what purposes? To win votes for devious politicians, who are likely to find they have done nothing to improve their levels of trust with the public in this way; and to gain publicity and status for lobbyists, journalists, talk-back hosts and so on whose careers thrive on its existence.

There are, however, *natural limits* to how far any penal system can accommodate populist demands, as we are beginning to see in the United States. The rate of imprisonment in Kentucky increased from 88 per 100,000 of population in 1970 to 423 in 2003. By this juncture, the state had simply run out of money to pay for these levels of imprisonment. Despite opposition from criminal justice officials and the local press, the state governor ordered the immediate release of nearly 1,000 felons. Lawson (2004: 5) writes that:

> [F]or the first time in twenty five years, driven to some extent by . . . harsh economic conditions in state budgets, law and policy makers have begun to manifest some serious concerns over the masses of humanity in the prison systems and to question the soundness of tough-on-crime policies that work to overload a corrections system that is already bulging at every seam. There is . . . thus an opportunity for an enlightened debate over whether the country is well-served by laws and policies that fill to capacity all the prisons and jails the nation can build in pursuit of a belief that harsh and long prison sentences are indispensable to public order and public safety.

Similarly, Jacobson (2005: 213) cites the examples of California, Connecticut and Louisiana, where there have been attempts (usually in the form of cutting back on mandatory sentencing and taking a more relaxed attitude to lesser parole violations) to reduce prison numbers. This has been driven by political and economic necessities, which then raise the possibilities of penal reform: 'the states are all in different levels of financial distress, with California experiencing the worst fiscal problems in the country, Connecticut has suffered its own financial crisis and Louisiana has endured a period of financial constraint.'

In other words, when the ultimate limits that there are to state budgets have been reached, this then shifts the terms of penal debate in such a way as to undercut the power and dominance of populism. When penal populism begins to adversely touch on the lives of ordinary people – in these examples by threatening closure of schools and hospitals, or leaving them chronically under-funded to pay for prisons – then public support for it, and the political will to carry it through, may begin to retreat. *This is penal populism's Achilles heel.* It is intended to punish those who threaten the well-being of ordinary people, not deprive ordinary people of what they expect the state to provide for them.

6

IS PENAL POPULISM INEVITABLE?

There are limits, then, to penal populism. Nor is it the only force at work on penal strategy and thought. However, given that its origins lie in deep seated social structural change across late modern society as a whole rather than mere local political opportunism, does this then mean that penal populism is an inevitable characteristic of late modernity?[1]

The answer to this question is that it has become a very prevalent characteristic of late modern society, but it is not an inevitable one. There are modern societies where it has not been able to make headway because their social arrangements act as barriers to it. However, as current indicators in these same societies suggest, these barriers are not impermeable. Even so, this does not then mean that there is no possibility of resistance to penal populism. However, for this resistance to have any purchase, it must fit the new terms of penal debate that have provided the opportunity for penal populism to flourish.

BARRIERS TO POPULISM

We can ascertain the form that these barriers can take by examining how three societies – Canada, Germany and Finland – remained resistant to penal populism as it gained strength elsewhere.

Canada

If the globalization of knowledge and ideas was indeed such an automated process, then Canada, as the United States' northern neighbour should have been among the first to follow its penal example. Its rate of imprisonment should now be amongst those that bear the closest correspondence to that of the United States, 738 per 100,000 of population. Yet remarkably, its prison population has been in decline – from a rate of 131 per 100,000 of population in 1995 to 107 in 2003. What seems to have happened in this country is what Meyer and O'Malley (2005: 214) refer to as a 'glocalizing reaction' to the United States' trends: that is, the assertion of regional or national autonomy in the face of global pressures. There seems to have been a widespread consensus in Canadian political and bureaucratic circles that the United States' crime control options have been a disaster and should not be repeated in Canada. This has meant that, in relation to penal policy, populist strategies have been able to make little headway there. While the simplistic and guileful slogans – three strikes, zero tolerance and so on – which emanate from penal development in the United States have been flashed around the world (Franko Aas 2005), Canada has had the benefit of more old fashioned neighbourly communication with that country and sees its realities very clearly. As a result, it prefers a 'Canadian way' of dealing with social problems, in much the same way that it wants other aspects of Canadian life to reflect the identity of that country rather than the United States (Meyer and O'Malley 2005: 211).

How though has it been able to achieve this? On the face of it, many of the preconditions for penal populism are present in Canada. As we have seen, the decline in deference has been just as strong in Canada as elsewhere. The fragmentation of longstanding pillars of support and stability have also taken place in that country. Canadian public opinion on crime and punishment issues seems to be much the same as for the rest of the anglophone world: most Canadians still think crime is increasing when in fact it has been in decline since 1991; most Canadians think that the courts are too lenient, a view which has changed little in 25 years (Roberts *et al.* 2003: 28–9). In their survey of 17 industrialized countries, van Kesteren *et al.* (2000: 85) found that although most Canadians feel safe going out alone at night, a relatively high number have burglar alarms and safety locks in their homes. In addition, Canadians were amongst the most punitive in these seventeen societies, with one of the most marked switches in support for imprisonment since 1989 (ibid.: 87–89). It may well be the case, as Meyer and O'Malley (2005: 211) argue, that there has been no public support for the abandonment of Canada's commitment to rehabilitation in favour of a more punitive reorientation in its prisons. In reality, though, such public opinion ambiguities seem no different from those in similar societies where penal populism has become entrenched.

For example, in the United Kingdom between 71 and 74 percent of the public between 1987 and 2001 thought that the courts were too lenient and not punitive enough (Roberts *et al.* 2003). Yet in 2000, 56 percent of those asked disagreed with the question 'Prison works: the more prisons the better.'[2] Equally in New Zealand, nearly 92 percent of voters supported the 1999 law and order referendum. Yet in the aftermath of the speech by the Leader of the Opposition in which, *inter alia*, he promised to virtually abolish parole and increase the prison population by another 50 percent (Brash 2004), an opinion poll found that 56 percent of those surveyed actually supported parole when accompanied by appropriate levels of community supervision;[3] similarly an opinion poll in 2006 found that 56 percent of those surveyed favoured spending more on community punishments rather than prisons.[4]

If, then, public opinion is not more ostensibly liberal and tolerant from that in similar societies where penal populism has been able to make significant headway, why is it that Canada has been able to avoid populist influenced policy? A good part of the explanation for this relates to *the political determination* in Canada to eschew the United States example, irrespective of public opinion poll findings that suggest there might be some popular resonance with it. This determination has allowed penal values from the different cultures in that country to have a significant influence. Canada has become well known for her restorative justice developments, often modelled on the practices of her First Nation peoples. There has also been the francophone influence from Quebec, a province whose penal policies and values are less punitive than those in most of anglophonic Canada (Tonry 2006: 17). At the same time, the Correctional Service of Canada seems to be a particularly authoritative central state bureaucracy. It not only has a strong commitment to correctional reform through rehabilitation, but is also associated with internationally recognized expertise in this area – Paul Gendreau and James Bonta, for example.[5] This would also indicate that Canadian governments, at least, have faith in their home grown experts and are prepared to look inwards to them to provide solutions to penal problems. This is in contrast to trends in those societies where populism is strong: there, expertise is likely to be downgraded and uninformed public sentiment and opinion given more weight.

Furthermore, Canadian governments – certainly at federal level – seem to have been able to successfully give the impression that they are being tough on crime and thereby assuaging any populist ripples when in reality they are doing the opposite. For example, youth justice legislation in 2003 designed to reduce the level of custody was presented as increasing custodial terms:

> [T]hat appeared to be the result of motivated 'leaks' from the government. It was clear that leaks – or at least the stories that resulted from what we believe to be motivated government leaks – were successful in convincing the public ... that the soon-to-be-released law was 'tough'.
>
> (Doob and Sprott 2006: 228)

Canada's penal bureaucracies and related organizations also seem to have skilfully managed the presentation of crime data and research findings in such a way as to minimize any tendency toward populist vendettas (Meyer and O'Malley 2005: 211). Notwithstanding the potential of findings in a government sponsored victimization survey in 2001 that 'on average 31 percent of adult Canadians reported being afraid of crime' to create sensational headlines, when releasing this information, the Solicitor General's Office reported that 'most Canadians feel safe in their communities. Conveying these findings to the public is important to counter-balance media portrayals of crime as a pervasive problem' (quoted by Meyer and O'Malley 2005: 211). Instead of allowing the information to be presented as 'nearly one third of Canadians feel unsafe in their homes', as might have been the case with a more supine bureaucratic organization, it affirmed instead that:

> Dealing with crime is not seen as a high government priority. In a recent survey, only 2 percent of respondents saw crime as an

area that the government should focus on, far behind issues of
health care, education and the economy.

(ibid.)

The Canadian democratic structure presents another barrier
to populism. This consists of federal and provincial systems
of government, with each tier having its own penal bureaucracy. In addition, responsibility for penal affairs is divided
between federal and provincial governments: the former
maintain penitentiaries, housing all those offenders serving
sentences of two or more years; the latter maintain jails for
those serving less than two years. Penal authority is thus
both diffused and at the same time a long way removed from
the agitations of any local law and order associations. Before
these can make any headway they have to pass through
successive layers of government and bureaucracy, a considerable test of endurance for what are usually loosely held
together coalitions. There is a very marked contrast here
with New Zealand where populism has been able to have so
much success. This country has a unicameral system of government and only one penal bureaucracy. This allows for a
much clearer demarcation of penal power and also provides
the possibility for much more direct access to governments
by populist organizations (Pratt and Clark 2005). The
Canadian system of government also differs in these respects
from that of the United States. There, crime and punishment issues are likely to be given much greater attention at
state level, where there is greater jurisdiction over these
matters, but rather less in other areas of government, allowing again for greater local influence of law and order lobby
groups.

The role played by the state in generating a strong civic
culture provides another barrier. Notwithstanding progressive cutbacks from the mid 1980s (Battle 1998), social
welfare provision seems to have been more extensive than

that provided in similar anglophone countries (see Castles 1996, for example), with little dismantling of state responsibilities and no significant switch from public to private providers. In these respects, the state remains a guarantor of security and stability, avoiding the attendant anxieties that restructuring has caused in other societies, where the state welfare role – but not its penal role – has been restricted and limited. Where this has happened, citizens have had to grasp that their fate is very much in their own hands, with little state protection from external forces that might threaten it. Amidst the atomized social arrangements that then prevail, they not surprisingly become suspicious and alert to all those 'others' who are thought to harbour such threats. In contrast, the enhanced presence of the Canadian state may have led to greater levels of public civility and trust.

Finally, the journalistic integrity of its national broadcasting company – the Canadian Broadcasting Corporation – has been largely maintained, notwithstanding the restructuring over the last decade that has forced it to be more dependent on advertising revenue. It has thus been able to resist law and order headline-grabbing approaches to reporting and provides opportunities for more informed public debate, instead of endless tabloid television. At the same time, it remains a very popular Canadian institution (Ryan 2006).

Germany

In this country, imprisonment rates fell during the 1970s. They have remained stable since then (Tonry 2004b), around the 2005 rate of 96 per 100,000 of population. One likely reason for this is that, for much of the post-war period, Germany also developed *and maintained* an extensive welfare state. Based around compulsory social insurance rather than means tested social assistance, it was designed to provide status preservation via earnings related transfer payments (Leibfried and Obinger 2003). There was little restructuring and contracting out of these responsibilities (Zedner 1995). Provision of this kind is thus likely to have reduced welfare stigma, while at the same time providing an essential guarantee of stability and security. In England, in contrast, means tested welfare was always intended as a way of preventing destitution rather than maintaining living standards. Indeed, it still bears the imprint of the less eligibility principle, introduced by the 1834 Poor Law. This institutionalized a stigmatic distinction between deserving and undeserving poor in welfare administration which has remained ever since in that country. In contrast, in Germany, the post-1945 welfare state was regarded as a nation builder rather than a failure (see p. 53).

Another reason for the stability of prison levels in Germany in an era of rising imprisonment is likely to have been the nature of crime reporting in that country. Zedner (1995: 522) wrote that:

> In Germany . . . the mass of traditional crimes which so pre-occupy in Britain draw comparatively little media coverage. Crime-related stories occupy much less space in press, radio and television reporting and, as a consequence, attract less political attention and fewer resources.

Furthermore, during the 1990s, fear of crime was at a relatively low level, while trust in criminal justice organizations was high (Oberwittler 2003). This is related to the high level of deference to and respect for criminal justice experts and judges in that country. German law professors, for example, played a large role in writing that country's penal code in the 1960s. Reflecting on this, Tonry (2004b: 1205) writes that 'in England or America, the idea that policy makers would regularly consult the views of law professors and even give deference to them and their authority would startle most observers.'

At the same time, prosecutors and judges are members of a career cadre (Tonry 2006) which is supported by the belief that their decisions should be protected from political influence and that judges and prosecutors will also be positive influences on policy processes. In part, this respect seems to be the product of the different legal training and occupational status of judges in most of continental Europe when compared to the anglophone world. As Lappi-Seppälä (2006: 71) writes, 'countries with trained professional judges and where criminology is included in the curriculum of law faculties may expect to have judges and prosecutors who have broader and deeper understanding of issues such as crime and criminal policy.' As a result of the public confidence in criminal justice professionals that this brings about, there do not seem to be any pressures in Germany or other European societies to introduce sentencing advisory bodies with the power to give detailed instructions on what sanctions should be imposed for which offences (ibid.). It is possible, of course, as has happened with the English Sentencing Guidelines Council (which unusually but probably significantly, has a judicial majority in its membership [8 / 12]), that the elected or politically nominated representatives of such bodies may actually advise a reduction of sentencing norms,[6] but as a general rule, there is surely a much greater risk that these bodies will recommend increased penalties, once they have to incorporate the views of victims groups and other representatives of public opinion. In contrast, it is as if judges in countries such as Germany are regarded as highly specialized technocrats, needing no obtrusive accountability processes or democratic scrutiny: unlike in the United States where judges, as elected officials, are always accountable to the public and subject to attendant political influences; and unlike other anglophone countries where they are seen as a privileged elite, out of touch with reality and public expectations. It may also be, of course, that the legacy of Nazi Germany has since led to a determination to uphold *the independence* of the judiciary and leave it free from any interference in the name of 'the people'-

Finland

The deference to law professors and other members of the criminal justice establishment is probably even stronger in this country. Having said this, it is also the case that Finnish sentencing practices are highly structured, 'with detailed provisions on the general principles and specific criteria to be taken into account in deciding both on the type and amount of punishment' (Lappi-Seppälä 2006: 7): this then acts as a shield against outside political pressures. Furthermore, Lappi-Seppälä (2000: 37) writes that Finnish society is 'exceptionally expert-oriented. Reforms have been prepared and conducted by a relatively small group of experts whose thinking on crime policy ... has followed similar lines.' He is referring here to the role they played in engineering the remarkable drop in the Finnish prison population from a rate of around 200 per 100,000 of population in 1950 to 55 per 100,000 in 1998. This was achieved through the implementation of strategies which included depenalization, decriminalization and the provision of effective alternatives to custody. In addition, government organizations, particularly the quasi-autonomous National Research Institute of Legal Policy, under the direction of Patrik Törnudd for much of this time, carefully managed information for public release, taking care to avoid controversy. The most significant law professor involved in this process of reform was Inkeri Antilla, the first woman to hold such a position at the University of Helsinki. She also served a term as Minister of Justice in the 1970s and was again the first woman to do so. As evidence of the esteem in which she is held in this country, a special medal was struck in her honour to mark her 80th birthday in 1996. The President of Finland wrote as follows of being taught by her:

> I had the privilege of studying law at the University of Helsinki under Inkeri Antilla . . . her relentless efforts for a more humane criminal justice system were based on the gathering of facts, awareness of both failures and successes in other countries, and above all a careful weighing of the pros and cons of alternative courses of action. *That is the best antidote against populism.*
>
> (Lahti and Törnudd 2001: preface, my italics)

These comments illustrate the coalition of interest that still exists in Finland between political elites and intellectuals: rather than being seen as alien outsiders, the ideas of the latter are valued and are influential on policy development.

At the same time, the Finnish system of government – a unicameral parliament with a single penal bureaucracy – ironically very similar to that of New Zealand – provides the opportunity for individuals to make radical changes to policy where there is not the depth of governance characteristic of Canadian society. In contrast to New Zealand, where vociferous spokespeople for law and order organizations have used these opportunities, liberal elites have taken these opportunities from the 1960s, with diametrically opposed results. Furthermore, trust in social and political institutions in Finland is amongst the highest in Europe (Lappi-Seppälä 2006). This level of trust has not occurred by accident but has been historically embedded. Trust in the legal profession came about because of the strong belief developed in the nineteenth century in legal structures and written law as guarantees of Finnish autonomy – Finland at that time was part of the Russian Empire, with the status of a self-ruling Grand Duchy. In addition, artists and intellectuals played an important part in strengthening Finnish national identity from this time. The 'debt of honour' that this has led to has since become an entrenched feature of the culture of that country. Wandering around her capital city, Helsinki, one finds numerous statues of intellectuals, economists, artists and musicians, with streets and parks named after them – a further example of the way in which these qualities are celebrated and respected in this country, in contrast to the veneration of ignorance over intellect that is associated with populism.

These cultural barriers are to be found elsewhere in Scandinavia. Sweden demonstrates the value it has for the intelligentsia by awarding Nobel prizes for the highest achievements in arts and science; similarly Norway awards Nobel peace prizes. We would not expect to find countries where such values are celebrated to be able to tolerate high levels of imprisonment or degrading conditions within them. Trust and tolerance have also been cemented in to Finnish and other Nordic societies through the development of extensive welfare state provision, designed to offset any tendencies towards social marginalization and inequality: nobody is to be excluded. Marklund and Nordlund (1999: 33) observe that:

> Denmark, Finland, Norway and Sweden do constitute a group that differs from other nations with respect to expenditure for social welfare, tax rates, large public service sectors, a large public transfer sector and a more active labour market policy. There are also indicators to show that the income distribution is more even and that poverty levels are lower.

Welfare takes the form of universal provision in these countries, rather than serving as a residual safety net. If welfare is understood in the latter more restricted and stigmatic way, it is likely to find few allies when neo-liberal governments cut it back and transfer responsibilities for its provision from the state to the private sector. In contrast, Finland and its

Scandinavian neighbours have been resilient welfare states with:

> [M]any more defenders than enemies during the 1990s. The number of defenders exceeded that of attackers by many times because these welfare states were designed to benefit everybody. When cutbacks are made in encompassing welfare states, they concern everybody.
>
> (Timonen 2003: 191)

In these respects, the inclusive model of state welfare provision again provides high levels of stability and security and allows it to act as a shock absorber in times of dramatic social change, without the distrust and lack of faith that this has brought about elsewhere. For example, Finland suffered a deep recession in the early 1990s with unemployment reaching 20 percent, but this made no impact on levels of disorder, inspired no populist resentment against the government nor produced any rises in imprisonment.

The state's guarantee of well-being extends to victims of crime in this country. It compensates them and then attempts to recover this from criminals. In this way, there is the opportunity for closure for victims, in so far as this is possible. This stands in marked contrast to those countries where there are now reparation schemes between victim and offender, with the state dropping out of proceedings. What these processes can lead to is the prolongation of victimization, to little benefit or gain: only 18 percent of reparation orders in New Zealand are adhered to. The sense of disenchantment and disillusionment that is likely to be the consequence feeds into support for penal populism and allows victimization to be politicized: victims become prizes to be fought over by politicians who try to outbid each other with the promises they make to them. These usually take the form of tokenistic gifts, as with the New Zealand Prisoners and Victims Claims

Act, gestures that in reality are likely to effect no more than a handful of victims, rather than the systemic and universal provision for them in Finland.

Finland has also been a very homogeneous society: its immigration rate of 2 percent is much lower than the other Scandinavian countries.[7] This has meant that there are no substantial ethnic minorities at the bottom of every social indicator who then achieve a disproportionate level of representation in prison (von Hofer 2003). Homogeneity also leads to trust and the building of interdependencies. This may then explain why there are such low levels of fear of crime in Finland. Only 4 percent of homes have burglar alarms: this compares with 34 percent in England (van Kesteren *et al.* 2000). At the same time, participation in neighbourhood watch, again indicative of a strong civic culture, has very high support (Bondeson 2005: 195).

The tabloid press in Finland plays a much less influential role in public affairs than in Britain and is less sensational than its equivalent in the other Scandinavian countries (Lappi-Seppälä 2006). State television continues largely unreconstructed, with no advertising and, although satellite channels are available, it maintains the highest audiences (ibid.). In contrast to the drama of *Crimewatch*, Lappi-Seppälä (ibid.: 64) observes that 'the Finnish version of Police-TV is more like an education programme with criminal justice officials explaining the contents and functions of the criminal justice system.' It may also have been that, until recently at least, the Finnish language structure provided insularity, with no global news media then available through satellite television or the Internet. When Finland looked outwards, it was east, towards Russia, or towards the other Scandinavian countries, as the counterweight to the eastern possibilities (Christie 1968); but it would seem that she did not look, had no need to look, beyond this region. She was able to develop her own solutions to social problems, with some regional influences but none from Britain or America.

This overview of penal developments in these three countries illustrates that barriers to populism are constructed out of local circumstances and histories – in just the same way that these may make a given society particularly vulnerable to populism.[8] Even though similar disembedding processes may be taking place in these three countries as those where populism is strong, there are features of their social structural and cultural arrangements which are able to offset these and shut populism out. At the same time, just as penal populism itself is not constructed from one single blueprint, nor are these barriers to it. The reasons for their emergence in one country will not be applicable in another. However, there have been at least three important commonalities shared by Canada, Germany and Finland. First, as penal populism became influential elsewhere, each had an entrenched and authoritative civil service that was largely in control of penal events in these countries. Second, their respective media was able to contribute to *informed public debate*: sources of public information are not dominated by tabloid television and press, as they tend to be where penal populism is strong. Third, their respective welfare provisions provided solidity and stability. This in turn is likely to foster trust and interdependencies between individual citizens, providing the possibilities for what Putnam (2000: 21) has referred to as 'generalized reciprocity'. This involves the following:

> I'll do this for you without expecting anything specific back from you, in the confident expectation that someone else will do something for me down the road. A society characterized by generalized reciprocity is more efficient than a distrustful society, for the same reason that money is more efficient than barter. If we don't have to balance every exchange instantly, we can get a lot more accomplished. Trustworthiness lubricates

social life. Frequent interaction among a diverse set of people tends to produce a norm of generalised reciprocity.

However, in many modern societies, the institutions which were once able to provide this 'social capital' have fragmented. The fear, resentment and suspicion that this leads to have then provided openings which allow populism to thrive. In contrast, the welfare arrangements of Canada, Germany and Finland have been able to prevent this, or to at least offset such consequences. Ironically, it seems to be the absence of something close to Putnam's reciprocity concept that the British government holds responsible for the growth of incivilities and lack of respect in that country. The Ministerial foreword to the Home Office (2003: 6) White Paper *Respect and Responsibility* claims that:

> Our aim is a something for something society where we treat one another with respect and where we all share responsibility for taking a stand against what is unacceptable. But some people and some families undermine this. The anti-social behaviour of a few damages the lives of many.

However, cultures of reciprocity and respect which then act as barriers to populism are more likely to take effect when they emerge from deeply embedded, inclusionary social networks. They are less likely to materialize when they are demanded as a moral imperative by politicians who themselves command little respect, and whose populist policies lead to further divisions in the social body rather than providing for its unification.

CRACKS IN THE WALL

Nonetheless, there are signs — very clear signs in some respects — which suggest that these barriers are beginning to crack. As regards Canada, the federal election of 2006 brought the Conservative Party to power with a neo-liberal economic agenda. This seems likely to bring about more restructuring of that country's welfare and taxation system, imposing additional limits on the former, fewer burdens but greater divisions as regards the latter. At the same time, law and order issues were prominent in that election and were sparked by one particular incident – the murder of a 15-year-old girl who got caught up in a shootout between rival gangs in downtown Toronto on 26 December 2005. One of the consequences was that 'the Conservatives promised to increase mandatory jail sentences for gun crimes, end statutory release of prisoners after serving two thirds of their sentences, and to press for a constitutional amendment to bar prison inmates from voting' (Parsons 2006: 2). Given the sharp ideological shift to the right that the electoral success of the Conservative Party represents in Canada, the federal political understandings and arrangements which had previously blocked populism may now be in jeopardy.

As regards Germany, Tonry (2004b: 1205) writes ominously that 'the professoriate now has much less influence and that these things are changing.' Not only this, but a familiar picture regarding public knowledge of crime is emerging now in this country. Recorded crime has been in decline since the early 1990s, yet Germans grossly overestimate their crime rate, while fear of crime is increasing (Clark and Wildner 2000). The reason for this disjunction seems clear: the German media has begun to follow a pattern of crime reporting that is similar to the anglophone world.[9] At the same time, welfare security is being redrawn and more thinly measured out: 'wage earners at risk will increasingly have to rely on the market and/or means-tested benefits and cannot depend any longer on the state alone' (Leibfried and Obinger 2003: 42). The social democratic consensus underpinning its welfare arrangements received a major blow in the federal election of 2005. This brought the Conservative Democratic Union to power, albeit as head of a grand coalition. Piece by piece unravelling of the welfare state in that country seems certain to continue.

In Finland, and in the other Scandinavian countries, prison populations are increasing, notwithstanding that they still remain some significant distance behind most other Western countries: from a rate of 55 per 100,000 of population in 1998 to 74 in Finland in 2005; from 56 to 68 in Norway; 69 to 78 in Denmark; 58 to 78 in Sweden. At the same time, their unique welfare arrangements have also been cut back (although not fundamentally redrawn). First, because of financial constraints:

> Internal developments have forced politicians and administrators to rethink some aspects of the welfare state. Ageing of populations, changes in family stability and gender relations and changes in the organisation of work are the most important internal factors that power the push for reforms. In most political speeches the state of the public economy and dependency ratios have become the most crucial question for the future of the welfare state.
>
> (Kautto *et al.* 1999: 3)

Second, because of European Union harmonization of welfare and social policies.[10] European Union membership has led to 'stringent demands regarding deficits, debt inflation and interest rates which placed additional pressures on social spending' (Timonen 2003: 7). Harmonization not only begins to shake the pillars on which social order in these countries has been built, but moves are being made to extend it to the penal realm, with the likelihood of undermining Scandinavian liberal traditions: 'harmonisation (more severe penalties) is needed because of the "changing nature of crime" in order to "prevent jurisdiction shopping" and to "remove the safe havens" of crime' (Lappi-Seppälä 2004: 5). The method so far chosen in sanction harmonization has been to set minimum levels for maximum penalties. This re-writing of crime control policies to counter new forms of crime – highly organized, planned, even to the point of picking 'soft' countries with liberal penal systems to use as the base for their crimes – may well have a knock-on effect in elevating penalties for more mundane crimes. Furthermore, the way in which such policies seem to undermine national autonomy may then give strength to any nascent populism.

At the same time, the globalization of news and information inevitably seeps through the autonomy and insularity of a society such as Finland. The language of populism is known here and the other Scandinavian countries, even if it is not yet widely spoken – certainly not in Finland. In many ways, though, the Scandinavian countries may become victims of their own successes. High standards of education have meant that most of their citizens have a good, if not excellent understanding of English. This obviously has the potential to make them more accessible to anglophone culture and values – including its very different approaches to punishment.

In Finland, the rise in imprisonment has been the result of changing attitudes to drug, sexual and violent crime, brought about by changing compositions in the penal elites and a more active role by some Conservative politicians. However, the situation has now stabilized and the control of prison rates has again become one of the major strategic policy goals of the Ministry of Justice (Lappi-Seppälä 2006). In contrast, populism is making more recognizable headway in Denmark and Sweden. As one of the telltale signs, expert knowledge may now find itself surplus to policy making requirements in these two countries. In 2002, the Danish Prime Minister thus announced in his traditional New Year speech to the nation that:

> We do not need experts or arbiters of taste to rule for us ... A tyranny of experts tends to suppress the free debate of the public. The Danish people should not have to listen to so-called experts who feel that they know best. Experts may be good at relating to us their factual knowledge; but faced with personal choices, we are all experts.
>
> (quoted by Balvig 2004: 169)

As the Swedish anti-drugs policy has been introduced (see p. 95), 'those questioning [it] are being portrayed as constituting *the* threat to the deterioration of the drugs situation, *rather than economic and social processes taking place within society*' (Tham 2005: 14, my italics). What are these 'economic and social processes'? The former include compliance with European Union harmonization requirements and the more general reorganization of welfare priorities taking place in Sweden. The latter include changing patterns of immigration, which destabilize the homogeneity of this region, causing the greatest turbulence to date in Denmark. The Danish People's Party gained seats in the 2006 election, amidst fears that Danish national identity was being undermined by European Union enlargement and by the more general movement of peoples from east to west and south to north that is characteristic of the twenty-first century. The message of the Danish People's Party is a simple but very powerful one: 'We want our old Denmark back' is the cry of one of its MP's (quoted by Rydgren 2004: 486). Similar cries can be heard across Europe. In Greece, unwelcome Albanians generate hostilities just as unwelcome Moslim immigrants do in Denmark. Archimandritou (2005: 3) writes that:

> Homogeneity played a crucial role [in developing informal nets of social control] until recently but the 1990s has been the fatal decade for the great transformation of Greek society. Unexpected immigration flows from neighbouring countries

have resulted in higher crime rates, unresolved social problems and new questions that require elaborate answers. This has been a new challenge for a society that some decades ago used to send immigrants to other places of the world.

In conjunction, the Greek rate of imprisonment increased from 55 per 100,000 in 1998 to 82 in 2005. In the Netherlands, the rate of imprisonment has increased from 85 per 100,000 of population in 1998 to 127 in 2005. This has taken place amidst 'lingering apprehensions about the Dutch multi-cultural society . . . and issues of immigration, integration, and the over-representation of ethnic minorities in the criminal justice system' (Pakes 2004: 285).

THE SORCERER'S APPRENTICE REVISITED

The barriers to populism are thus not impermeable. Even in the three societies and similar others where they have proved effective in the past, it is possible to discern breaches in them, or at least the potential for breaches to occur. This does not mean that the barriers in these societies are in danger of imminent collapse. What it does indicate, though, is that there is no natural immunity to populism. Instead, where there is immunity, this is likely to have been built up from long standing social arrangements and deeply embedded cultural values. However, when these are rearranged or begin to fragment, immunity levels decrease and the opportunities for populism increase. Thereafter, the route back to those previous social arrangements that provided immunity is unclear – if one exists at all. Meanwhile, as penal populism seizes these opportunities, it becomes very difficult to eradicate.

What then happens is that penal strategy and thought, instead of being driven primarily by concerns about efficiency, economy and humanitarianism, has to incorporate, and is sometimes overwhelmed by, the emotive forces that populism unleashes. Of course, restorative justice advocates will argue that letting emotions loose in the criminal justice arena is to be welcomed. They see remorse and shame on the part of offenders, forgiveness and forbearance on the part of victims. This may be so, but the predominant emotions swirling around contemporary penal debate seem much more likely to be those of fear and intolerance, suspicion and anger: precisely because of the social conditions which have allowed these emotions to emerge at this juncture. Indeed, these emotions may become even more taut and strained. First, because the social conditions which have made their release possible seem to be accelerating and cutting more deeply into the foundation structures of Western society as a whole. Second, as we see in those countries where penal populism has already had significant effect, it creates expect-ations of security and order that are almost always disap-pointed. Promises of returns to fabled crime-free eras can never materialize, because they are nothing more than fables.

In this way populism victimizes and re-victimizes all those 'ordinary people' in whose name it claims to speak. All those ordinary people whose hopes are unrealistically built up with promises of ever longer, ever tougher sentences, only to find that the realities are some measure short of the unremitting absolutism that had been promised. All those ordinary people whose fears about rapists and murderers being paroled have been unnecessarily raised, because in reality they will never be granted it. However, their victims or their families are encouraged to live through such events all over again by making their own representations to parole boards, a right that is usually given to them (although many probably never asked for or wanted it) by proud populist politicians. The anger and the disillusionment this creates when there is no closure, no satisfaction, no relief, is unlikely to be directed back at the forces of populism – after all, these have become the great hope of the disenchanted. These contain too much moral investment to be tarnished by their own failures. Instead, such feelings are likely to be redirected at the experts who still seem to stand in the way of the will of the people. In effect, populism's own failures may only help to refuel it.

Under these circumstances, it can gather a momentum that then becomes very difficult to apprehend. Indeed, in some jurisdictions, politicians have lost control over what they have helped to create, reminiscent of von Goethe's (1797) fable, *The Sorcerer's Apprentice*. The apprentice used magic to make a broomstick come to life and perform the work he had been ordered to do by the sorcerer. At first, the magic was very successful but then, with increasing panic and alarm, the apprentice realizes he has no way of bringing under control what he has let loose. The more he tries to arrest it, the more chaos the broomstick makes. The moral of the fable is a simple one: *do not start something without knowing how to stop it*. Similarly, those politicians who help to bring penal populism to life by invoking magic spells such as 'tough on crime, tough on the causes of crime', initially welcome the electoral success it brings them. They then find, however, that they too have no magic words to make it stop, as they begin to recoil from the havoc it creates. Thus the lament of the New Zealand Corrections Minister that 'we lock people up at the second-highest rate [in the OECD] and that is pretty terrible really' (*The Press* 3 May 2006: 1).

Are there, though, any magic spells to bring it under control, or do we simply have to let it run its course until it exhausts all the resources necessary to fuel it, coming to a halt at some remote point on a far-drawn penal horizon? Rather than waiting for such eventualities and the damage that may be done in the meantime, and given the way in which many of the assumptions in which penal populism is founded are palpably false, cannot the entire edifice be brought crashing down by demonstrating these falsities? Assumptions about increasing crime rates, assumptions about supposedly luxurious prison conditions, assumptions about lenient sentencing, assumptions about public opinion and punishment. As Roberts *et al.* (2003) have demonstrated, public opinion on sentencing – the sentencing of actual cases rather than general comment – is nothing like so unremittingly unforgiving as populists make it out to be. However, as they go on to state (ibid.: 174), academics have failed to engage effectively with this debate and have proved unable to develop persuasive alternatives to penal populism. Why cannot this conflicting evidence burst the populist balloon? They write that (ibid.: 163) 'unfortunately, the research qualifying the general conclusions that the public are punitive is seldom referred to in debates about the future of sentencing.'

In point of fact, this disjuncture *is* regularly referred to in *academic* debate; it is usually the case, however, that there is simply no space for this in *public* debate. As Haggerty (2004: 221) puts the matter, 'as political discourse becomes more televisual and emotive, the rational print-based evidence and arguments . . . of academic criminologists are apt to play a reduced role on the political stage.' Rationality – the continuous restating of arguments about prison costs, lack of effectiveness, reconviction rates and so on – that were the kernel of policy under the previous axis of penal power – will not prevail in and of itself. It is exactly this kind of detailed, informed knowledge which might be effective in changing opinions under experimental research conditions with focus groups, but which is so difficult to fit within more general modes of public discourse and communication. As Indermaur and Hough (2002: 210) acknowledge, 'the appeal of simplified and tough minded penal policy lies in its ability to resonate with public emotions such as fear and anger . . . Anyone who wants to improve public debate about crime needs to be attuned to this emotional dimension.'

Nor is it simply the case of ensuring that those with

liberal credentials are placed in positions of power and influence. As Ryan (2003) has illustrated, there are already numerous people in such positions. In Britain, for example, successive Chief Inspectors of Prisons have been amongst the fiercest critics of populist excesses and their effects on prison conditions. Yet Sir David Ramsbottom, on his retirement, commented on his five years' work that 'I have never received ministerial acknowledgement of, or response to any of [my annual] reports or their contents or their recommendations' (*The Weekly Telegraph* 31 July 2001: 10). It is not, then, that there is a lack of this critical information. What needs to be reassessed is the way such information is presented and packaged.

The work of the *Rethinking Crime and Punishment Programme* set up by the Esmeé Fairburn Foundation in Britain has been one way in which academics and penal reformers have tried to make this engagement more effective. It sought to raise the level of public debate about penal affairs by undertaking media work, public education campaigns and staging events to raise public consciousness (Allen 2004). It is surprising, though, that little consideration has been given to the use of scandal – events which contravene all the known local limits of penal sensibilities – by those in opposition to populism. Sparks (2000: 133) writes of scandal that '*particular events*, stories and controversies can in their aftermath exercise profound effects, both at the level of popular consciousness and of political, legislative and system level change.' Scandal has become the almost exclusive property of populists. They make great play of what they see as scandals – for them, punishments that are insufficiently punitive – in their attempts to undermine the criminal justice establishment. However, *penal policy which is too severe* also provokes scandal: it, too, contravenes penal sensibilities. Brown (2005) thus notes that the Northern Territory Punitive Work legislation (see p. 31) was repealed after four years following a series of popular campaigns utilizing emotion and anger against punitiveness. Similarly in relation to prison conditions. Control units in English prisons, introduced in the mid 1970s, were closed after one year due to public outrage. There have also been scandals over the detention conditions and treatment of pregnant women prisoners in England. At one point, these women were being chained to hospital beds:

> The Home Office was forced to end the practice after [the Chairwoman of the Association for Improvements in Maternity Services] took a camera into the Whittington hospital in London and photographed a Holloway prisoner being shackled an hour after giving birth. The pictures were shown across the media and caused a furore.[11]

Inevitably, such engagements are likely to be *ad hoc*, contingent and unpredictable. Furthermore, such attempts to challenge populism and undermine public support for it are subject to the whims of the media, which becomes a necessary adjunct to them. When the author of the 1999 New Zealand referendum question (*not* the organizer of the referendum itself, Norm Withers) was sentenced to nine years imprisonment in 2005 for sexual offences against minors, it might be thought that it was scandalous for such a person to have been allowed so much influence on penal policy. It should then follow that there would be the opportunity to discredit the referendum itself, one of the foundation stones of penal populism in this country. However, attempts to do so have come to nothing.[12] Clearly, scandal works best when it is concentrated around the here and now rather than incidental events that took place several years earlier. The referendum might stand out as a glaring light in the memories of academics; for the general public however, it has probably long faded into oblivion.

Nonetheless, the convergence of several incidents in New

Zealand *have had* sufficient force to scandalize and thereby attract the interest of the media, particularly journalists and television reporters working in crucial opinion-forming positions in it. First, the cost of four new prisons currently being built (the cost of one might have gone unnoticed), vastly in excess of what was originally budgeted, at a time when public expenditure is under pressure in areas that have more utility has become a matter of public debate.[13] Second, there have been two authoritative reports, including one from the respected Salvation Army (Smith and Robinson 2006), which carries no discrediting establishment baggage, highlighting the enforced idleness and the absence of work or education for most prisoners in this country.[14] This information undercuts public expectations that prison expenditure should have *some* purpose, whether it be hard labour or rehabilitation: to spend so much money to no effect – *to keep most prisoners doing nothing whatsoever* – generates considerable public agitation. Third, New Zealand's high rate of imprisonment – 189 per 100,000 of population – is beginning to become an inscribed feature of political and public debate, since it so clearly challenges the reputation for egalitarianism and social justice that is also associated with this country (Pratt 2005). This convergence has thus helped to rewrite the way in which prison can be 'scandalized' in this country. It no longer focuses exclusively on escapes and luxuries – although it still does focus on these when provided with appropriate opportunities – but also asks what such levels of imprisonment, what such prison conditions, are saying about New Zealand as a society.

In 2006, the public interest that had been provoked in this way encouraged a commercial television station – TV3 – to make and screen a programme in primetime which very unfavourably compared the New Zealand prison system with that of Finland – thereby giving the scandal more food and energy.[15] In its aftermath, the country's two leading newspapers have run features on the problems of New Zealand's prisons,[16] even if the reporting has been somewhat schizophrenic at times. For example, in the same edition of *The Dominion Post* (28 February 2006), the front page headline was: 'Jail lets sex crims out to pick fruit.' This event was reported as a scandal that would fuel populism. In reality, sex offenders had been given day release to pick fruit on local farms at a time of acute labour shortages. Meanwhile the editorial (at B4) explained that:

> New Zealand has proved itself very good at locking up criminals. It is what is happening after the prison door slams that is an unacceptable failure ... society needs to look again at how it deals with its criminals, and look at it more urgently.

Now the paper was addressing a different kind of prison scandal – one provoked by the very attitudes and style of reporting displayed on its front page.

What will be the outcome of the intense penal debates being conducted in this country remains unclear. But that such debates *are taking place* demonstrates that there are effective ways to challenge populism and that there can be resistance to it. However, to mount such resistance, it is vital that those in the academy become actively engaged in public and political discourse themselves. In the introduction to this book, we saw that the concept of penal populism has found its way into everyday discourse and is being addressed at this level by politicians, journalists and significant others. It is all the more important, as Ryan (2005: 147) argues, for those in the academy to lobby '*outwards* rather than *inwards*' and participate in such debates. If they choose not to, then they will remain on the sidelines, hapless observers of the populist forces that the new axis of penal power has forged and let loose.

NOTES

CHAPTER 1

1   Nor is this populism confined to Western Europe. In the former communist block, once the new-found freedoms of capitalism have been found to be illusory, then there have been reversions to electoral support for populist parties which are anti the new establishment that has grown up since the collapse of communism. They look for solutions to unemployment and widening gaps between rich and poor that this has brought about through the desire for strong political leadership, as in the case of Romania and the rise of the Great Romania Party (Mungiu-Pippidi 2001).

2   On the basis of Lewis (1997), it may well have been the latter. The book indicates that Howard's sojourn at the Home Office always seemed to be a stepping stone to higher things – hence, in the manner of a populist politician, his care to cultivate public support and popularity while there.

3   The article, written by the paper's political editor was titled 'Us and Them, and they've got no idea.'

4   Reported crime in New Zealand fell from a high of 520,000 offences in 1994 to 390,000 in 2005.

5   For example, in the United States, the National Crime Commission reported in 1967 that:

America must translate its well-founded alarm about crime into social actions that will prevent crime. It has no doubt whatever that the most significant action that can be taken against crime is action designed to eliminate slums and ghettos, to improve education, to provide jobs, to make sure that every American is given the opportunities and the freedoms that will enable him to assume his responsibilities.

(Caplan 1973: 591)

6   This figure must be understood in the context of New Zealand's total population of 4.1 million.

7   This was a gross misrepresentation, based on the increase between the number of convictions for homicide (2) in 1962 and the number of murders in 2001 (80). However, this claim came to be accepted in public and political debate and was never publicly challenged.

8   The form that this notification takes varies from state to state. For example, in Minnesota, 90 days prior to being released from prison, sex offenders are assigned to one of three risk levels (for those who are thought to constitute a severe risk, the Department of Corrections or Police can still petition to have them civilly committed anyway). It is those who are thought to be most seriously at risk – risk level three – that the consequences of notification are broadest and most serious: 'local law enforcement, victims, witnesses and any agencies that serve a population at risk of victimization may be notified, as well as the general public.' Community notification to the public may take place in the form of a community meeting. People living within a three block radius of where the offender will be or is residing may receive notice of the community meeting via a flyer and/or by City watch, a telephone broadcast system designed to send residents a recorded message about an upcoming meeting (http://www.ci.minneapolis.mn.us/police/crime-prevention/sex-offenders.asp). Failure to comply with notification procedures, such as changing address without permission, is considered a felony. However, risk level three offenders in Nebraska are publicized to a much wider audience:

in addition to notifying local law enforcement, schools, day care centers and religious and youth organizations, the public will be notified through news releases directed to the media within the state. Additional news releases, community meetings, or direct contact with neighbours may be utilized by the local law enforcement to provide notice in addition to the state patrol news release.

(Klasskids.org/st-neb.htm)

CHAPTER 2

1 In Canada, the rate of criminal code incidents declined from 10,342 criminal incidents per 100,000 of population in 1991 to 8,051 in 2004; in New Zealand, recorded crime decreased from 525,622 offences in 1991 to 390,000 in 2005; in the United States it decreased from 29,745,766 recorded offences in 1991 to 23,390,528 in 2004. In England recorded crime fell from 5,591,717 offences in 1992 to 4,481,817 in 1999. Since then, there have been changes in counting procedures breaking the running statistical record. Nonetheless, with the current practice of combining police statistics and British Crime Survey findings, it has been calculated that the risk of victimization declined from 40 percent in 1995 to 24 percent in 2005, the lowest level since the British Crime Survey began in 1981 (Nichols *et al*. 2005). See also Tonry (2005) for more specific detail and also declines in crime rates in continental Europe.

2 In Canada, the rate of criminal code incidents increased from 2,771 per 100,000 of population in 1962 to 10,342 in 1991; in England, the level of recorded crime increased from 743,713 offences in 1960 to 5,276,173 in 1991; in New Zealand, recorded crime increased from 102,792 offences in 1960 to 525,622 in 1991; in the United States it increased from 3,384,200 in 1960 to 29,745,766 in 1991.

3 As in most of the English speaking world, civil servants in New Zealand are prohibited from speaking publicly about such matters, even though in this particular setting, their comments may be publicly reported.

4 He was almost certainly right. The two wealthiest constituencies returned the lowest level of 'yes' votes – 77.5 percent and 81.33 percent respectively.

5 British Cabinet Minister, Patricia Hewitt (2005: 1) has referred to this as 'a very good thing, particularly in a country where social relations have been so distorted by an old deeply entrenched class system.'

6 For example, numbers of tertiary students increased from 15,809 in 1960 to 132,396 in 2002 in New Zealand; in Australia from 53,780 to 896,621; in the United States from 3,216,000 to 15,928,000 (*New Zealand Yearbook* 1962, 2004; *Yearbook of the Commonwealth of Australia* 1962, 2003; *United States Statistical Abstract* 1976, 2005, United States Census Bureau 1976, United States Census Bureau 2005).

7 For example, in New Zealand and New South Wales, the first full-time probation officers and prison psychologists were not appointed until the 1950s. Furthermore, there had still been little opportunity to implement the rehabilitative ideal before its 'collapse' in the mid 1970s.

8 See: http:sentencingcommission.alacourt/.gov/about.html:7

9 There is a clear division between the 'residual model' of the welfare state characteristic of the anglophone world which acts as a 'safety net' and little more than this for the needy who are also stigmatized by becoming a burden on the state, and the 'institutional model' characteristic of the Scandinavian countries where all citizens are entitled to wide ranging benefits and services, thereby creating 'a solid basis of support for the welfare state among all income groups and . . . a high degree of equality of both incomes and opportunities' (Esping-Andersen 1990: 27). The role of the Scandinavian welfare state in providing a barrier to the inroads of penal populism will be considered in detail in Chapter 6.

10 *People and Politics*, BBC World Service.

11 See: http://en.wikipedia.org/wiki/Black_Wednesday.html

CHAPTER 3

1 For example, TV New Zealand and the Canadian Broadcasting Company (CBC).

2 For example, 'Inquiry into fiasco of killer's early release . . . murderer freed despite 91 percent risk he would offend again' (see: http://www.guardian.co.uk/crime/article/0,2763,1669488,00.html).

3 See http://www.atschool.eduweb.co.uk/stevemoss/bron/ayer.htm. It might be thought that the BBC's contemporary *Question Time* is an obvious successor. However, its panellists are usually politicians who then most usually answer political questions.

4 Cook (2002: 140–1) writes in relation to Television New Zealand that 'the average length of a news item has reduced by approximately 20 seconds (90 and 70) between 1984 and 1996.' At the same time, the maximum length of any news item fell from nine minutes in 1984 to four minutes thirty seconds in 1996.

5 SST spokesperson Garth McVicar thus accompanied the New Zealand Corrections Minister on a fact finding trip to Europe January/February 2006, albeit with his liberal counterpart from the Prison Fellowship Trust.

6 For example, 'Mr McVicar gives no credence to those warm and fuzzy criminologists and civil liberties types who say [his SST organization] has too much clout. "I don't apologize for driving the debate at all", he said' (*The Dominion Post* 17 December 2005: B4).

7 As Crofts (2004: 262) puts the matter:

> The immediacy of news reporting and interviews with ordinary people 'just like us' – publicans, neighbours, eyewitnesses and . . . grieving friends and relatives – underscores the immediacy of violent threat to our everyday lives, and leaves us ample space to identify as fearful victims of crime ourselves or as closely connected to victims.

8 Non-ideal victims will receive far less coverage: 'if the victim is male, working class, of African, Caribbean or Asian descent, a persistent runaway, has been in care, has drug problems or is a prostitute . . . reporters perceive that the audience is less likely to relate to or empathise with [them]' (Jewkes 2004: 52).

9 Sarah Payne was another such victim; as was Norm Withers' mother, attacked while minding his shop as he had lunch. Defenceless, innocent and randomly and brutally attacked, if she could be victimized, then the entire community could be victimized (see Pratt and Clark 2005). Two-year-old James Bulger was also such a victim (see Chapter 4).

10 This was actress Winona Ryder, who offered a $US200,000 reward for her return (see Domanick 2004: 118).

11 See the comments of Dr Don Brash, p. 17.

12 The rate of imprisonment in the United States rose from 490 to 710 per 100,000 of population during Clinton's tenure of office.

CHAPTER 4

1 See: http://www.news10.net/storyfull1.asp?id=12619

2 In the New Zealand Sentencing Act 2002, the sentence of preventive detention is available for 'first strike' sexual offenders aged 18 and over.

3 My italics, see: http://www.lamonitor.com/articles/2005/08/18/headline.news/news01.txt

4 I am indebted to Terry Thomas for directing me to this mosaic. For a flavour of these issues, see for example, *The Independent* (4 November 1995) on the West case; *The Independent* (17 January 1996: 4), 'Sex abuse and fraud at home run by Christians'; *The Scotsman* (9 June 1997: 6), 'Paedophile on the prowl but police are powerless to act'; *The Yorkshire Post* (23 November 1996: 2), ' "Dreadful" scandal of sex terror'; *The Guardian* (20 April 1996: 5), 'Sex attacker pounces on schoolgirl returning to class'; *The Guardian* (7 November 1995: 11), ' "Court too lenient" on rapist, 14'; see also Lippens (2004) on the Dutroux case.

5 See Hacking (1992), for example.

6 Crime and Disorder Act 1998, s.34.

7 A paraphrase of Prime Minister John Major's comments on this case, reported in *The Mail on Sunday* (21 February 1993: 1).

8 The Court of Appeal then ruled Howard's intervention unlawful and it was then quashed by the House of Lords after Judicial Review in 1997; Taylor LCJ imposed a minimum term of ten years after a ruling from the European Court of Human Rights in December 1999. This followed a ruling that judges rather than the Home Secretary should determine jail terms for juvenile killers.

9 3 CrAppR (S) 245 (my italics); reaffirmed in R v Bailey (1988) 10 CrAppR (S) 231.

10 Hansard HOC 8 April 1998, vol. 370.

11 '. . . respect the old for what it [sic] still has to teach, respect for others, honour, self discipline, duty, obligations, the essential decency of the British character,' this really should come as no surprise to us', Women's Institute speech 2000, quoted at http://politics.guardian.co.uk/queensspeech2005/story/0,16013,1486296,00.html

12 As this was being written in 2005, plans were already afoot to cleanse Auckland of such pollutants when it hosts the Rugby World Cup in 2011.

CHAPTER 5

1 See Kant (1797 (1965)) and Hart (1968).

2 R v Secretary of State for the Home Department, ex parte Doody (1994) 1 AC 531.

3 See, for example, Wynne v United Kingdom [1994] IIHRL 61 (18 July 1994), European Court of Human Rights (case no 26/1103/421/500); R v Secretary of State for the Home Department ex parte Allen [2000] 144 SJLB 152; R v Secretary of State for the Home Department, ex parte Hindley [2001] 1 AC 410.

4 Indeed, the American courts have shown a marked reluctance to decline the constitutionality of measures such as three strikes and sexual predator laws while taking a 'hands off' approach to developments in penal institutions (Haney and Zimbardo 1998). For case law, see pp. 29–30.

5 Quoted in *The Guardian* (10 December 2004: 3).

6 This was the thrust of the National Party's opposition to the Prisoners and Victims Claims Bill – that it was an elaborate charade by the Labour government to find a way round United Nations conventions on prisoners' rights and which would only enrich lawyers – the conventions should simply have been ignored and the government refuse to pay any damages to the prisoners (*The Holmes Show*, TV1, 16 September 2004).

7 On these various matters, see Pratt (2002).

8 In New Zealand, penalties involving supervision declined from 4,977 in 1994 to 1,900 in 2005, while work-related penalties declined from 30,183 to 25,103. Custodial sentences increased from 7,360 to 8,540 (Spiers and Lash 2004). In England, in the Crown Court, community penalties declined from 22,021 sentences in 1993 to 20,421 in 2004; sentences of immediate custody increased from 31,985 to 42,438. In Magistrates Courts, however, community penalties increased from 43,832 to 58,268: this, though, was largely at the expense of the fine (93,935 to 59,398) since sentences of immediate custody increased from 11,289 to 32,358 (Sentencing Guidelines Council 2006).

9 See Johnson (2002), Daly (2002). Restorative justice no longer seems to be the exclusive property of indigenous communities and 'new social movements' (Braithwaite 1989).

10 See *The Guardian* (20 April 2006: 3): '[Home Secretary to announce

"dangerous persons order". Emergency measures to control the movement of violent offenders after they leave prison will be announced . . . the new rules will include orders for violent offenders similar to those already applying to sex offenders.'

11 As regards New Zealand, see, for example, *The Dominion Post* (13 May 2005: 1):

> Parents fear paedophile in West Coast town. West Coast parents are fearing for their children's safety after police told a school a paedophile had moved there [the] District Mayor said today: 'there is no place for a person like that in a small community like Blackball [sic].'

The man was physically expelled from Blackball a day later, amidst the onlooking local crowd.

12 See, for example, Hermer and Mosher (2002) in relation to similar city ordinances in Canada.

13 A search of the two leading New Zealand newspapers from 2002 to 2005 revealed nine such cases, including one where the driver was found not guilty of sexual assault.

14 One such driver was 'sixteen years old when, thirty four years ago, he had sex with his girlfriend two days before her sixteenth birthday' (*The Dominion Post* 14 February 2006: 4).

15 Although the rise and comparative longevity of the New Zealand SST is something of an exception. See p. 27.

16 Zimring (1996: 244, my italics) thus writes of the California three strikes legislation that 'my general conclusion is that Three Strikes was an *extreme example* of populist preemption of criminal justice policy making. No outside proposal is likely to march through the legislative process untouched by human hands again soon.' As regards New Zealand, there was a 'perfect storm' that allowed penal populism to take the form it did. See Pratt and Clark (2005).

CHAPTER 6

1 Garland (2001: 141) writes that 'the [penal] policy-making process has become profoundly politicised and populist. Policy measures are constructed in ways that appear to value political advantage over the views of experts and the evidence of research.'

2 See: http://www.mori.com/polls/2000/2000poll.htm

3 *National News*, TV1, June 2004.

4 *Campbell Live*, TV3, 7 February 2006.

5 See, for example, Gendreau (1996), Bonta (1996). Both have worked for the Correctional Service of Canada, and both are included by Cullen (2005) amongst 'the twelve people who saved rehabilitation'; as is fellow Canadian Don Andrews.

6 *The Observer*, 12 March 2006; http://www.observer.guardian.co.uk/uk_news/story/0,1729136,00.html

7 The rate for Norway and Denmark is 8 percent per year; for Sweden it is 15 percent.

8 See Pratt and Clark (2005) in relation to New Zealand.

9 'Safer Streets, Growing Fear', 16 June 2005; http://www.dw.world.de/dw/article/0,2144,1617212,00.html

10 Denmark joined the EU in 1970, Sweden and Finland in 1995. Norway, while not a member of the EU, is part of the European Economic Area, which gives it access to the EU's internal market.

11 See: http://society.guardian.co.uk/crimeeandpunishment/story/0,1699147,00.html

12 The author has raised this issue with journalists on numerous occasions since this man's conviction in 2005, but they have never carried the story.

13 The current estimate for the cost of these prisons is $NZ890 million; it was originally $300 million in 2002.

14 For the second report, see Office of the Ombudsman (2005).

15 *Campbell Live*, 7 February 2006.

16 See *The New Zealand Herald*, 'Our Idle Jails' series, 25 February 2006 to 4 March 2006; *The Dominion Post*, 'Bulging Prisons Spark Rethink', 25 February 2006, A10.

BIBLIOGRAPHY

Allen, F. (1981) *The Decline of the Rehabilitative Ideal: Penal Policy and Social Purpose*, New Haven: Yale University Press.

Allen, R. (2004) 'What works in changing public attitudes – lessons from rethinking crime and punishment', *Journal for Crime, Conflict and the Media*, 1 (3): 55–67.

Allison, P. (1991) 'Stranger than fiction', *Metro Magazine*, June: 98–109.

Almond, G. and Verba, S. (1963) *The Civic Culture; Political Attitudes and Democracy in Five Nations*, Princeton, NJ: Princeton University Press.

Anderson, C. (1996) 'Economics, politics and foreigners: populist party support in Denmark and Norway', *Electoral Studies*, 15 (4): 497–511.

Anderson, D. (1995) *Crime and the Politics of Hysteria: How the Willie Horton Story Changed American Justice*, New York: Times Books.

Archimandritou, M. (2005) 'Public safety and risk society. Greece and the great expectation', unpublished paper.

Ashworth, A. and Hough, M. (1996) 'Sentencing and the climate of opinion', *Criminal Law Review*, 776–787.

Atkinson, J. (1993) 'Television deregulation and political discourse', *Mental Health News*, Autumn: 9–11.

Bai, M. (1997) 'A Report from the Front in the War on Predators', *Newsweek*, 129 (20): 67.

Baker, E. and Roberts, J. (2005) 'Globalization and the new punitiveness', in J. Pratt, D. Brown, S. Hallsworth, M. Brown and W. Morrison (eds) *The New Punitiveness: Trends, Theories, Perspectives*, Cullompton, UK: Willan Publishing.

Balvig, F. (2004) 'When law and order returned to Denmark', *Journal of Scandinavian Studies in Criminology and Crime Prevention*, 5: 167–187.

Barrett, D., Kurian, G. and Johnson, T. (eds) (2001) *World Christian Encyclopedia*, New York: Oxford University Press.

Bass, E. and Davis, L. (1988) *The Courage to Heal*, New York: Harper and Row.

Battle, K. (1998) 'Transformation: Canadian social policy since 1985', *Social Policy and Administration*, 32 (4): 321–340.

Bauman, Z. (1997) *Postmodernity and its Discontents*, Cambridge: Polity Press.

—— (2001) *Liquid Modernity*, Cambridge: Polity Press.

—— (2002) *Society Under Siege*, Cambridge: Polity Press.

—— (2004) *Wasted Lives: Modernity and its Outcasts*, Malden, MA: Blackwell.

Beckett, K. (1997) *Making Crime Pay: Law and Order in Contemporary American Politics*, New York: Oxford University Press.

—— (2005) 'Criminalizing space: the transformation of urban social control', paper presented at the 57th annual meeting of the American Society of Criminology, Toronto, Canada, November 2005.

Best, J. (1990) *Threatened Children*, Chicago: University of Chicago Press.

Betz, H.G. (1994) *Radical Right-Wing Populism in Western Europe*, Basingstoke, England: Macmillan.

Bird, S.E. (2000) 'Audience demands in a murderous market: tabloidization of U.S. television news', in C. Sparks and J. Tulloch (eds) *Tabloid Tales: Global Debates Over Media Standards*, Lanham, MD: Rowman & Littlefield Publishers.

Blair, T. (2005) *Our Citizens Should not Live in Fear*. Online. Available HTTP: http://politics.guardian.co.uk/comment/story/0,,1664712,00.html (accessed 15 April 2006).

Bondeson, U. (2005) 'Levels of punitiveness in Scandinavia: description and explanation', in J. Pratt, M. Brown, S. Hallsworth, M. Brown and W. Morrison (eds) *The New Punitiveness: Trends, Theories, Perspectives*, Cullompton, UK: Willan Publishing.

Bonta, J. (1996) 'Risk-needs assessment and treatment', in A.T. Harland (ed.) *Choosing Correctional Options that Work: Defining the Demand and Evaluating the Supply*, Thousand Oaks, CA: Sage.

Bottoms, A.E. (1977) 'Reflections on the renaissance of dangerousness', *Howard Journal of Criminal Justice*, 16: 70–96.

—— (1995) 'The Philosophy and Politics of Punishment and Sentencing', in C. Clarkson and R. Morgan (eds) *The Politics of Sentencing Reform*, Oxford: Clarendon.

Braithwaite, J. (1989) *Crime, Shame and Reintegration*, Cambridge: Cambridge University Press.

Braithwaite, J. and Parker, C. (1999) 'Restorative justice is republican justice', in G. Bazemore and L. Walgrave (eds), *Restorative Juvenile Justice: Repairing the Harm of Youth Crime*, Monsey, NY: Criminal Justice Press.

Brash, D. (2004) 'Law and Order – A National Priority', address given to the Sensible Sentencing Trust, Wellington, New Zealand, 4 July 2004.

Brattan, W.J. (1997) 'Crime is down in New York City: blame the police', in N. Dennis (ed.) *Zero Tolerance: Policing a Free Society*, London: The IEA Health and Welfare Unit.

Brown, D. (2005) 'Continuity, rupture or just more of the "volatile and contradictory"?: glimpses of New South Wales' penal practice behind and through the discursive', in J. Pratt, D. Brown, S. Hallsworth, M. Brown and W. Morrison (eds) *The New Punitiveness: Theories, Trends, Perspectives*, Cullompton, UK: Willan Publishing.

Bruce, S. (2000) *God is Dead: Secularization in the West*, Oxford: Blackwell Publishers.

Calabrese, A. (2000) 'Political space and the trade in television news', in C. Sparks and J. Tulloch (eds), *Tabloid Tales: Global Debates Over Media Standards*, Lanham, MD: Rowman & Littlefield Publishers.

Campbell, B. (1993) *Goliath: Britain's Dangerous Places*, London: Methuen.

Canovan, M. (1981) *Populism*, New York: Harcourt Brace Jovanovich.

—— (1999) 'Trust the people! populism and the two faces of democracy', *Political Studies*, 47: 2–16.

Caplan, G. (1973) 'Reflections on the nationalization of crime: 1964–8', *Law and the Social Order*, 19: 583–638.

Castles, F. (1996) 'Needs-based strategies of social protection in Australia and New Zealand', in G. Esping-Andersen (ed.) *Welfare States in Transition: National Adaptations in Global Economies*, London: Sage.

Cavadino, M. and Dignan, J. (2002) *The Penal System: An Introduction*, 3rd edn, London: Sage.

—— (2005) *Penal Systems: A Comparative Approach*, London: Sage.

Central Statistical Office (2002) *Social Trends: A Publication of the Government Statistical Service*, London: HMSO.

Chibnall, S. (1977) *Law and Order News: An Analysis of Crime Reporting in the British Press*, London: Tavistock Publications.

Christie, N. (1968) 'Aspects of social control in welfare states', in N. Christie (ed.) *Scandinavian Studies in Criminology*, vol. 2, Oslo: Universitetsforlaget.

—— (2004) *A Suitable Amount of Crime*, New York: Routledge.

Citizens' Forum on Canada's Future (1991) *Citizen's Forum on Canada's Future: Report to the People and Government of Canada*, Ottawa: Supply and Services Canada.

Clark, D.E. and Wildner, M. (2000) 'Violence and fear of violence in East and West Germany', *Social Science and Medicine*, 51 (3): 373–379.

Cohen, S. (1985) *Visions of Social Control: Crime, Punishment, and Classification*, Cambridge: Polity Press.

Cook, D. (2002) 'Deregulation and broadcast news content: ONE network news 1984 to 1996', in J. Farnsworth and I. Hutchinson (eds) *New Zealand Television: A Reader*, Palmerston North, NZ: Dunmore Press.

Crawford, A. (2006) 'Institutionalizing restorative youth justice in a cold, punitive climate', in I. Aertsen, T. Daems, and L. Robert (eds) *Institutionalizing Restorative Justice*, Cullompton, UK: Willan Publishing.

Crawford, A. and Newburn, T. (2002) 'Recent developments in restorative justice for young people in England and Wales. Community participation and representation', *British Journal of Criminology*, 42: 476–495.

Crist, C. (1996) 'Chain gangs are right for Florida', *Corrections Today*, 58: 178.

Cross, B. (2000) *Members of Parliament, Voters and Democracy in the Canadian House of Commons*, Ottawa: Canadian Study of Parliament Group.

Cullen, F. (2005) 'The twelve people who saved rehabilitation: how the science of criminology made a difference', *Criminology*, 43 (1): 1–42.

Cumberbatch, G., Woods, S. and Maguire, A. (1995) *Crime in the News: Television, Radio and Newspapers: A Report for BBC Broadcasting Research*, Birmingham, UK: Aston University Communications Research Group.

Daly, K. (2002) 'Restorative justice: the real story', *Punishment and Society*, 4: 55–79.

Davies, M. (1985) 'Determinate sentencing reform in California and its impact on the penal system', *British Journal of Criminology*, 25: 1–30.

Davis, M. (1992) *City of Quartz: Excavating the Future in Los Angeles*, New York: Vintage Books.

de Raadt, J., Hollanders, D. and Krouwel, A. (2004) *Varieties of Populism: An Analysis of the Programmatic Character of Six European Parties*, Working Papers in Political Science No. 2004/04. Amsterdam: Vrije Universiteit.

Delli Carpini, M. and Williams, B. (2001) 'Let us infotain you: politics in the new media environment', in W.L. Bennett and R. Entman (eds) *Mediated Politics, Communication in the Future of Democracy*, Cambridge: Cambridge University Press.

Dession, G. (1937) 'Psychiatry and the conditioning of criminal justice', *Yale Law Journal*, 47: 319–340.

Dickey, W.J. and Smith, M.E. (1998) *Dangerous Opportunity: Five Futures for Community Corrections: The Report from the Focus Group*, Washington, DC: US Department of Justice, Office of Justice Programs.

Ditton, J. and Duffy, J. (1983) 'Bias in the newspaper reporting of crime news', *British Journal of Criminology*, 23: 159–165.

Domanick, J. (2004) *Cruel Justice: Three Strikes and the Politics of Crime in America's Golden State*, Berkeley: University of California Press.

Doob, A.N. and Sprott, J.B. (2006) 'Punishing youth crime in Canada: the blind men and the elephant', *Punishment and Society*, 8 (2): 223–233.

Dorfman, L., Woodruff, K., Chavez, V. and Wallack, L. (1997) 'Youth and violence on local television news in California', *American Journal of Public Health*, 87 (8): 1311–1316.

Douglas, M. (1966) *Purity and Danger*, London: Routledge and Kegan Paul.

Downes, D. and Morgan, R. (1997) 'Dumping the "hostages to fortune"?

The politics of law and order in post-war Britain', in M. Maguire, R. Morgan and R. Reiner (eds) *The Oxford Handbook of Criminology*, 2nd edn, Oxford: Oxford University Press.

Doyle, A. (2003) *Arresting Images: Crime and Policing in front of the Television Camera*, Toronto: Toronto University Press.

Duffy, B. (2003) *Who Do We Trust?* Online. Available HTTP: www.mori.com/publications/rd/trust.shtml (accessed 8 May 2006).

Dunbar, I. and Langdon, A. (1998) *Tough Justice: Security and Penal Policy in the 1990's*, London: Blackstone.

Durkheim, E. (1893) *De la Division du Travail Social*; trans. G. Simpson (1964) *The Division of Labor in Society*, New York: Free Press.

Ericson, R.V., Baranek, P.M. and Chan, J.B.L (1991) *Representing Order: Crime, Law, and Justice on the News Media*, Buckingham, UK: Open University Press.

Esping-Andersen, G. (1990) *The Three Worlds of Welfare Capitalism*, Princeton, N.J.: Princeton University Press.

European Commission (2004) *Standard Eurobarometer 61*, Brussels: Public Opinion Analysis Sector, European Commission.

Evans, J. (2003) 'Vigilance and vigilantes: thinking psychoanalytically about anti-paedophile action', *Theoretical Criminology*, 7: 163–189.

Fallows, J. (1997) *Breaking the News*, New York: Vintage.

Feely, M. and Simon, J. (1992) 'The new penology: notes on the emerging strategy of corrections and its implications', *Criminology* 30: 449–474.

Finkelhor, D. (1984) *Child Sexual Abuse: New Theory and Research*, New York: Free Press.

Finn, D. (1987) *Training Without Jobs: New Deals and Broken Promises*, London: Macmillan.

Fogel, D. (1975) *We are the Living Proof: The Justice Model for Corrections*, Cincinnati: W.H. Anderson.

Franko Aas, K. (2005) 'The ad and the form: punitiveness and technological culture', in J. Pratt, D. Brown, S. Hallsworth, M. Brown and W. Morrison (eds) *The New Punitiveness: Trends, Theories, Perspectives*, Cullompton, UK: Willan Publishing.

Freiberg, A. (2000) 'Guerrillas in our midst? Judicial responses to governing the dangerous', in M. Brown and J. Pratt (eds) *Dangerous Offenders*, London: Routledge.

—— (2003) 'The four pillars of justice: a review essay', *Australian and New Zealand Journal of Criminology*, 36 (2): 223–230.

Fukuyama, F. (1995) *Trust: The Social Virtues and the Creation of Prosperity*, New York: Free Press.

Fulton Committee (1968) *The Civil Service*, London: HMSO.

Furedi, F. (2001) *Paranoid Parenting*, London: Cappella Publishing.

Furedi, F. (2004) *Therapy Culture*, Oxford: Blackwell.

Gallup Organization (2005) *Confidence in Institutions*, Princeton, NJ: The Gallup Organization.

Garland, D. (1996). 'The Limits of the sovereign state: strategies of crime control in contemporary society', *British Journal of Criminology*, 36: 445–471.

—— (2001) *The Culture of Control*, New York: Oxford University Press.

Garvey, S. (1998) 'Can shaming punishments educate?', *University of Chicago Law Review*, 65: 733–794.

Gaubatz, K.T. (1995) *Crime in the Public Mind*, Ann Arbor, MI: University of Michigan Press.

Gendreau, P. (1996) 'The principals of effective intervention with offenders', in A.T. Harland (ed.) *Choosing Correctional Options that Work: Defining the Demand and Evaluating the Supply*, Thousand Oaks, CA: Sage.

Georgia Department of Corrections (1996) *Georgia Department of Corrections Annual Report 1996*, Atlanta, GA: Office of Public Affairs, Georgia Department of Corrections.

Giddens, A. (1990) *The Consequences of Modernity*, Stanford, CA: Stanford University Press.

—— (1991) *Modernity and Self-Identity*, Cambridge: Polity Press.

—— (ed.) (2001) *Sociology: Introductory Readings*, Oxford: Polity Press.

—— (2002) *Runaway World: How Globalization is Reshaping our Lives*, London: Profile Books Limited.

Girling, E., Loader, I. and Sparks, R. (1998) 'A telling tale: a case of vigilantism and its aftermath in an English town', *British Journal of Sociology*, 49 (3): 474–490.

—— (2000) 'After affluence?: the anxieties of affluence in an English village', in T. Hope and R. Sparks (eds) *Crime, Risk and Insecurity*, London: Routledge.

Gostomski, C. (1997) 'A case of "immoral conduct" ', *York Daily Record*, 13 July 1997.

Greenlees, L. (1991) 'Washington State's sexually violent predators act: model or mistake', *American Criminal Law Review*, 29: 107–132.

Hacking, I. (1992) 'World-making by king-making: child abuse for example', in M. Douglas and D. Hull (eds) *How Classification Works: Nelson Goodman among the Social Sciences*, Edinburgh: Edinburgh University Press.

Haggerty, K. (2004) 'Displaced expertise: three constraints on the policy relevance of criminological thought', *Theoretical Criminology*, 8 (2): 211–231.

Hall, S. (1979) *Drifting into a Law and Order Society*, London: Cobden Trust.

—— (1988) *The Hard Road to Renewal: Thatcherism and the Crisis of the Left*, London: Verso.

Hall, S., Critcher, C., Jefferson, T., Clarke, J. and Roberts, B. (1978) *Policing the Crisis: Mugging, the State, and Law and Order*, London: Macmillan.

Haney, C. and Zimbardo, P.G. (1998) 'The past and future of U.S. prison policy twenty-five years after the Stanford prison experiment', *American Psychologist*, 53 (7): 709–727.

Hansen, R., Bill, L. and Pease, K. (2003) 'Nuisance offenders: scooping the public policy problems', in M. Tonry (ed.) *Confronting Crime: Crime Control Policy under New Labour*, Cullompton, UK: Willan Publishing.

Harrison, P. (1983) *Inside the Inner City: Life under the Cutting Edge*, Harmondsworth, UK: Penguin.

Hart, H.L.A. (1968) *Punishment and Responsibility: Essays in the Philosophy of Law*, Oxford: Clarendon.

Held, D., McGrew, A.D., Goldblatt, D. and Perraton, J. (1999) *Global Transformations: Politics, Economics and Culture*, Oxford: Polity Press.

Hennessey, P. (1989) 'The Civil Service', in D. Kavanagh and A. Seldon (eds) *The Thatcher Effect*, Oxford: Clarendon Press.

Herrner, J. and Mosher, J. (eds) (2002) *Disorderly People: Law and the Politics of Exclusion in Ontario*, Halifax: Fernwood Publishing.

Hewitt, P. (2005) 'Britain Speaks', speech given at the Britain Speaks – Effective Public Engagement and Better Decision Making Conference, London 2005.

Hinds, L. and Daly, K. (2001) 'The war on sex offenders: community notification in perspective', *Australian and New Zealand Journal of Criminology*, 34: 256–276.

Hogeveen, B.R. (2005) 'If we are tough on crime, if we punish crime, then people get the message: constructing and governing the punishable young offender in Canada during the late 1990s', *Punishment and Society*, 7: 73–89.

Hogg, R. and Brown, D. (1998) *Rethinking Law and Order*, Sydney: Pluto Press.

Home Office (1996) *Protecting the Public: The Government's Strategy on Crime in England and Wales*, Cmnd. 3190, London: HMSO.

—— (1997) *No More Excuses: A New Approach to Tackling Youth Crime in England and Wales*, Cmnd. 3809, London: HMSO.

—— (2001) *Criminal Justice: The Way Ahead*, Cmnd. 5074, London: HMSO. Online.

—— (2002) *Justice for All*, Cmnd. 5563, London: HMSO.

—— (2003) *Respect and Responsibility – Taking a Stand Against Anti-Social Behaviour*, Cmnd. 5578, London: HMSO.

Hough, M. (1996) 'People talking about punishment', *Howard Journal of Criminal Justice*, 35: 191–214.

—— (1998) *Attitudes to Punishment: Findings from the 1992 British Crime Survey*, Social Science Research Papers no. 7, London: South Bank University.

—— (2003) 'Modernization and public opinion: some criminal justice paradoxes', *Contemporary Politics*, 9 (2): 143–155.

Hough, M. and Roberts, J.V. (1998) *Attitudes to Punishment: Findings from the British Crime Survey*, Home Office Research Study 179, London: Home Office Research, Development and Statistics Directorate.

—— (2004) *Confidence in Justice: An International Review*, London: Institute for Criminal Policy Research, King's College London.

House of Commons Home Affairs Committee (1993) *Juvenile Offenders: Sixth Report together with Proceedings of the Home Affairs Committee*, London: HMSO.

—— (2005) *Anti-Social Behaviour: Fifth Report of Session 2004–2005*, vol. 1, London: HMSO.

House of Lords (1996) 572, col.1049.

Hoyle, C. (2002) 'Securing restorative justice for the non-participating victims', in C. Hoyle and R. Young (eds) *New Visions of Crime Victims*, Oxford: Hart Publishing.

Hudson, B. (1987) *Justice through Punishment: A Critique of the 'Justice' Model of Corrections*, Basingstoke, UK: Macmillan.

Hutton, W. (1995) *The State We're In*, London: Jonathan Cape.

Indermaur, D. and Hough, M. (2002) 'Strategies for changing public attitudes to punishment', in J. Roberts and M. Hough (eds) *Changing Attitudes to Punishment: Public Opinion, Crime and Justice.* Cullompton, UK: Willan Publishing.

Inglehart, R. (1977) *The Silent Revolution: Changing Values and Political Styles Among Western Publics*, Princeton, NJ: Princeton University Press.

—— (1999) 'Trust, well-being and democracy', in M. Warren (ed.) *Democracy and Trust*, Cambridge: Cambridge University Press.

Jacobson, M. (2005) *Downsizing Prisons: How to Reduce Crime and End Mass Incarceration*, New York: New York University Press.

Jenkins, P. (1998) *Moral Panic: Changing Concepts of the Child Molester in Modern America*, New Haven: Yale University Press.

Jewkes, Y. (2004) *Media and Crime*, London: Sage.

Johnson, G. (2002) *Restorative Justice: Ideas, Values, Debates*, Cullompton, UK: Willan Publishing.

Johnston, L. (1996) 'What is vigilantism?', *British Journal of Criminology*, 36: 220–236.

Kant, I. (1797) *The Metaphysical Elements of Justice*; trans. John Ladd (1965) *The Metaphysical Elements of Justice; Part I of the Metaphysics of Morals*, Indianapolis: Bobbs-Merrill.

Kautto, M., Heikkilä, M., Hvinden, B., Marklund, S. and Ploug, N. (eds) (1999) *Nordic Social Policy: Changing Welfare States*, London: Routledge.

Kellner, P. and Crowther-Hunt, N. (1980) *The Civil Servants: An Inquiry into Britain's Ruling Class*, London: Macdonald Futura.

Kelsall, R.K. (1955) *Higher Civil Servants in Britain: From 1870 to the Present Day*, London: Routledge & Kegan Paul.

Kempe, R. and Kempe, C. (1978) *Child Abuse*, Cambridge: Harvard University Press.

King, R. (1999) 'The rise and rise of supermax: an American solution in search of a problem?', *Punishment and Society*, 1: 163–186.

LaFree, G. (1998) *Losing Legitimacy: Street Crime and the Decline of Social Institutions in America*, Boulder, CO: Westview Press.

—— (2002) 'Too much democracy or too much crime? Lessons from California's three-strikes laws', *Law and Social Inquiry*, 27 (4): 875–902.

Lahti, R. and Törnudd, P. (2001) (eds), *Inkeri Antilla. Ad Ius Criminale Humanius – Essays in Criminology, Criminal Justice and Public Policy*, Helsinki: Finnish Lawyers' Association.

Lappi-Seppälä, T. (2000) 'The fall of the Finnish Prison Population', *Journal of Scandinavian Studies in Criminology and Crime Prevention*, 1 (1): 27–40.

—— (2004) 'Nordic Systems facing the European Harmonization', paper presented at the Sovereign Criminal Law Systems and Integration from a Comparative Law Prospective Conference, Mexico 2004.

—— (2006) 'Penal policy in Scandinavia', in M. Tonry (ed.) *Crime and Justice: A Review of Research*, 34: Chicago: University of Chicago Press (in press).

Lawson, R.G. (2004) 'Difficult time in Kentucky corrections – aftershock of a "tough on crime" philosophy', *Kentucky Law Journal*, 93: 305–376.

Leibfried, S. and Obinger, H. (2003) 'The state of the welfare state: German social policy between macroeconomic retrenchment and micro-economic recalibration', *Western European Politics*, 26 (4): 199–218.

Lewis, D. (1997) *Hidden Agendas: Politics, Law and Disorder*, London: Hamish-Hamilton.

Lippens, R. (2004) 'Exhausting whiteness: the 1996–98 Belgian parliamentary inquiry into the handling of a paedophilia affair', in G. Gilligan and J. Pratt (eds) *Crime, Truth and Justice: Official Inquiry, Discourse, Knowledge*, Cullompton, UK: Willan Publishing.

Loader, I. (2005) 'Fall of the platonic guardians', *British Journal of Criminology*. Advance Access published October 7 2005, doi:10.1093/bjc/azi091.

London, J. (1903) *The People of the Abyss*, New York: Macmillan.

McEvoy, K. and Mika, H. (2002) 'Restorative justice and the critique of informalism in Northern Ireland', *British Journal of Criminology*, 43 (3): 534–563.

McLaughlin, E. (2001) 'Zero tolerance', in E. McLaughlin and J. Muncie (eds) *The Sage Dictionary of Criminology*, London: Sage.

Marklund, S. and Nordlund, A. (1999) 'Economic problems, welfare convergence and political instability', in M. Kautto, M. Heikkilä, B. Hvinden, S. Marklund and N. Ploug (eds) *Nordic Social Policy: Changing Welfare States*, London: Routledge.

Martinson, T. (1974) 'What works – questions and answers about prison reform', *The Public Interest*, 35: 22–54.

Matthews, R. (2005) 'The myth of punitiveness', *Theoretical Criminology*, 9: 175–201.

Mattinson, J. and Mirrlees-Black, C. (2000) *Attitude to Crime and Criminal Justice: Findings from the 1998 British Crime Survey*, Home Office Research Study No. 200, London: Home Office.

Mauer, M. (1999) *Race to Incarcerate*, New York: New Press.

Mayhew, P., Mirrlees-Black, C. and Aye Maung, N. (1994) *Trends in Crime: Findings from the 1994 British Crime Survey*, Home Office Research and Planning Unit Research Findings No. 14, London: Home Office.

Medina-Ariza, J. (2006) 'Politics of crime in Spain, 1978–2004', *Punishment and Society*, 8 (2): 183–201.

Meyer, J. and O'Malley, P. (2005) 'Missing the punitive turn? Canadian criminal justice, "balance" and penal modernism', in J. Pratt, D. Brown, S. Hallsworth, M. Brown and W. Morrison (eds) *The New Punitiveness: Trends, Theories, Perspectives*, Cullompton, UK: Willan Publishing.

Mika, H. and Zehr, H. (2003) 'A restorative framework for community justice practice', in K. McEvoy and T. Newburn (eds) *Criminology, Conflict Resolution and Restorative Justice*, New York: Palgrave MacMillan.

Miller, A. (1990) *The Day Care Dilemma*, New York: Insight Books.

Millie, A., Jacobson, J., McDonald, E. and Hough, M. (2005) *Anti-Social Behaviour Strategies: Finding a balance*. Bristol: Policy Press.

Ministerial Statement on the Criminal Justice System and Victims of Crime (1996), Darwin: Ministry of Justice.

Ministry of Justice (2002) *Reforming the Criminal Justice System*, Wellington: Ministry of Justice.

—— (2003) *Attitudes to Crime and Punishment: A New Zealand Study*, Wellington: Ministry of Justice.

Mirrlees-Black, C., Budd, T., Partridge, S. and Mayhew, P. (1998) *The 1998 British Crime Survey*, Home Office Statistical Bulletin 21/98, London: Home Office.

Morris, A. and Maxwell, G. (1993) 'Juvenile justice in New Zealand: a new paradigm', *Australian & New Zealand Journal of Criminology*, 26: 72–90.

Mountfield, R. (2000) *Civil Service Change in Britain*, speech given at the Political Studies Association Conference, London School of Economics, April 2000.

Muncie, J. (1999) 'Institutionalized intolerance: youth justice and the 1998 Crime and Disorder Act', *Critical Social Policy*, 19: 147–175.

Mungiu-Pippidi, A. (2001) 'The return of populism – the 2000 Romanian elections', *Government and Opposition*, 36: 230–252.

Nevitte, N. (1996) *The Decline of Difference: Canadian Value Change in Cross National Perspective*, Peterborough, Ontario: Broadview Press.

Newburn, T. (1997) 'Youth, crime, and justice', in M. Maguire, R. Morgan and R. Reiner (eds), *The Oxford Handbook of Criminology*, 2nd edn, Oxford: Oxford University Press.

—— (2002) 'Atlantic crossings: "policy transfer" and crime control in the USA and Britain', *Punishment and Society*, 4: 165–194.

Newburn, T. *et al.* (2002) *The Introduction of Referral Orders into the Youth Justice System: Final Report*, Home Office Research Study 242, London: Home Office Research, Development and Statistics Directorate.

Newburn, T. and Jones, T. (2005) 'Symbolic politics and penal populism: The long shadow of Willie Horton', *Crime, Media, Culture*, 1: 72–87.

Newsom, J. and Newsom, E. (1963) *Patterns of Infant Care*, London: Penguin.

New Zealand Government (2004) '*Prisoner comp legislation will aid victims*', media release, New Zealand Government, Wellington, 15 December.

New Zealand Year Book (1962) Government Printer: Wellington.

—— (2004) Government Printer: Wellington.

Nicholas, S., Povey, D., Walker, A. and Kershaw, C. (2005) *Crime in England and Wales 2004/2005*, London: Home Office.

North, R. (2003) *The Big Conversation: Whose Truth? Evidence, Trust and Policy in the 3rd Millennium*, Online. Available HTTP: www.richarddnorth.com/public_realm/evipol.htm (accessed 31 March 2006).

Oberwittler, D. (2003) 'The development of crime and the fear of crime in Germany – consequences for crime prevention', *German Journal of Urban Studies*, 42 (1): 31–52.

Office of the Ombudsman (2005) *Ombudsman's Investigation of the Department of Corrections in Relation to the Detention and Treatment of Prisoners*, Wellington: Office of the Ombudsman.

Office of the Press Secretary (1996) *Remarks by the President in Bill Signing Ceremony for Megan's Law*. Online. Available HTTP: <http://clinton6.nara.gov/1996/05/1996-05-17-president-remarks-at-signing-of-megans-law.html> (accessed 15 May 2006).

O'Malley, P. (2000) 'Criminologies of catastrophe? Understanding criminal justice on the edge of the new millennium', *Australian and New Zealand Journal of Criminology*, 33: 153–167.

Pakes, F. (2004) 'The Politics of Discontent: The Emergence of a New Criminal Justice Discourse', *Howard Journal of Criminal Justice*, 43 (3), 284–98.

Parker, P., Measham, F. and Alderidge, J. (1995) *Drugs Futures: Changing Patterns of Drug Use Among English Youth*, London: Institute for the Study of Drug Dependence (ISDD).

Parsons, L. (2006) 'The Canadian Elections and the Phony Gun-crime Epibid.ic', *World Socialist* Web site, www.wsws.org/articles/2006/jan2006/canaj17.shtml

Pearson, G. (1983) *Hooligan: A History of Respectable Fears*, London: Macmillan.

Pratt, J. (1998) *Governing the Dangerous*, Sydney: Federation Press.

—— (2002) *Punishment and Civilization: Penal Tolerance and Intolerance in Modern Society*, London: Sage.

—— (2005) 'The dark side of paradise', *British Journal of Criminology*. Advanced access published 1 November 2005, doi:10.1093/bjc/azi095.

Pratt, J. and Clark, M. (2005) 'Penal populism in New Zealand', *Punishment and Society*, 7: 303–322.

Pratt, J. and Treacher, P. (1988) 'Law and order and the 1987 New Zealand election', *Australian and New Zealand Journal of Criminology*, 21: 253–268.

Putnam, R.D. (2000) *Bowling Alone: The Collapse and Revival of American Community*, New York: Simon and Schuster.

Raphael, A. (1994) *Ultimate Risk*, London: Bantum Press.

Reiner, R. (2001) 'The rise of virtual vigilantism: crime reporting since World War II', *Criminal Justice Matters*, 43: 4–5.

Reiner, R. and Livingstone, S. (1997) *Discipline or Desubordination? Changing Media Images of Crime*. London: London School of Economics.

Report of the Department of Correctional Services (1985–86), Albany: Department of Correctional Services.

Report of the Prison Commissioners (1954), London: PP (1955–6), Cmd. 9547.

Roberts, J.V. (2002) 'Public opinion and the nature of community penalties: international findings', in J.V. Roberts and M. Hough (eds) *Changing Attitudes to Punishment: Public Opinion, Crime and Justice*, Cullompton, UK: Willan Publishing.

—— (2003) 'Sentencing reform in New Zealand: an analysis of the Sentencing Act 2002', *Australian and New Zealand Journal of Criminology*, 36: 249–271.

Roberts, J.V. and Stalans, L. (1997) *Public Opinion, Crime, and Criminal Justice*, Boulder, CO: Westview Press.

Roberts, J.V., Stalans, L., Indermaur, D. and Hough, M. (2003) *Penal Populism and Public Opinion*, New York: Oxford University Press.

Robinson, J., Young, W. and Haslett, S. (1990) *Surveying Crime*, Wellington, N.Z.: Institute of Criminology, Victoria University of Wellington.

Rock, P. (1990) *Helping victims of crime: the Home Office and the rise of victim support in England and Wales*, New York: Oxford University Press.

—— (1995) *Helping Victims of Crime*, Oxford: Clarenden Press.

—— (2004) *Constructing Victims Rights: The Home Office, New Labour, and Victims*, New York: Oxford University Press.

Roshier, R. (1973) 'The selection of crime news by the press', in S. Cohen and J. Young (eds) *The Manufacture of News; Social Problems, Deviance and the Mass Media*, London: Constable.

Rutherford, A. (1992) *Growing out of Crime: The New Era*, Winchester: Waterside Press.

Ryan, J. (2006) *Canadian 2006 Election: A Chilling Echo of Bush's Republicans*. Online. Available HTTP: www.globalresearch.ca (accessed 23 May 2006).

Ryan, M. (1978) *The Acceptable Pressure Group*, Farnborough: Saxon House.

—— (1999) 'Penal policy making towards the millennium: elites and populists, New Labour and the new criminology', *International Journal of the Sociology of Law*, 27: 1–22.

—— (2003) *Penal Policy and Political Culture in England and Wales*, Winchester: Waterside Press.

—— (2004) 'Red tops, populists and the irresistible rise of the public voice', *Journal for Crime, Conflict and the Media*, 1: 1–14.

—— (2005) 'Engaging with punitive attitudes towards crime and punishment: some strategic lessons from England and Wales', in J. Pratt, D. Brown, S. Hallsworth, M. Brown and W. Morrison (eds) *The New Punitiveness: Trends, Theories, Perspectives*, Cullompton, UK: Willan Publishing.

Rydgren, J. (2002) 'Radical right populism in Sweden: still a failure, but for how long?', *Scandinavian Political Studies*, 25 (1): 27–56.

Rydgren, J. (2004) 'Explaining the emergence of radical right-wing populist parties: the case of Denmark', *West European Politics*, 27 (3): 474–502.

Sampson, A. (1962) *Anatomy of Britain*, London: Hodder and Stoughton.

Savelsberg, J. (1994) 'Knowledge, domination and criminal punishment', *American Journal of Sociology*, 99: 911–943.

Scheingold, S. (1991) *The Politics of Street Crime: Criminal Process and Cultural Obsession*, Philadelphia, PA: Temple University Press.

Sennett, R. (2005) 'What our grannies taught us', *The Guardian*, 19 May 2005. Online. Available HTTP: http://politics.guardian.co.uk/comment/story/0,9115,1487272,00.html (accessed 21 April 2006).

Shearing, C. (2001) 'Transforming security: a South African experiment', in H. Strang and J. Braithwaite (eds) *Restorative Justice and Civil Society*, Cambridge: Cambridge University Press.

Shields, R. (1992) *Life-Style Shopping: The subject of consumption*, London: Routledge.

Shils, E. (1956) *The Torment of Secrecy*, London: Heinemann.

Simmons, J. and Dodd, T. (eds) (2003) *Crime in England and Wales 2002/2003*, London: Home Office, Research, Development and Statistics Directorate.

Simon, J. (1995) 'They died with their boots on: the boot camp and the limits of modern penality', *Social Justice*, 22: 25–49.

Skogan, W. (1992) *Disorder and Decline: Crime and the Spiral of Decay in American Neighborhoods*, Berkeley: University of California Press.

Smith, L. and Robinson, B. (2006) *Beyond the Holding Tank: Pathways to Rehabilitative and Restorative Prison Policy*, Manukau, NZ: The Salvation Army Social Policy and Parliamentary Unit.

Solomon, E. (2004) 'Crime policies – political orthodoxy fails', *The Legal Executive*, 16 December. Online. Available HTTP: www.ilexjournal.co.uk/ilexopinion/article.asp?theid=1002&themode=2 (accessed 5 May 2006).

Soothill, K., Francis, B. and Ackerley, E. (1998) 'Paedophilia and paedophiles', *New Law Journal*, 148: 882–883.

Sparks, R. (1994) 'Can prisons be legitimate? – penal politics, privatization, and the timeliness of an old idea', *British Journal of Criminology*, 34: 14–28.

—— (2000) 'Risk and blame in criminal justice controversies: British press coverage and official discourse on prison security (1993–6)', in M. Brown and J. Pratt (eds), *Dangerous Offenders. Punishment and Social Order*, London: Routledge.

—— (2001) ' "Bringin' it all back home": populism, media coverage and the dynamics of locality and globality in the politics of crime control', in K. Stenson and R. Sullivan (eds) *Crime, Risk and Justice: The Politics of Crime Control in Liberal Democracies*, Cullompton, UK: Willan Publishing.

Spiers, P. and Lash, B. (2004) *Conviction and Sentencing of Offenders in New Zealand: 1994–2003*, Wellington, NZ: Ministry of Justice.

Squires, P. and Stephen, D. (2005) *Rougher Justice*, Cullompton, UK: Willan Publishing.

Strang, H. (2002) *Repair or Revenge: Victims and Restorative Justice*, Oxford: Oxford University Press.

Surette, R. (1994) 'Predator criminals as media icons', in G. Barak (ed.) *Media, Process, and the Social Construction of Crime: Studies in Newsmaking Criminology*, New York: Garland Publishing.

Taggart, P. (2000) *Populism*, Milton Keynes: Open University Press.

Taylor, I. (1995) 'Private homes and public others: analysis of talk about crime in suburban south Manchester in the mid 1990s', *British Journal of Criminology*, 35: 263–285.

Taylor, I., Evans, K. and Fraser, P. (1996) *A Tale of Two Cities: Global Change, Local Feeling, and Everyday Life in the North of England*, London: Routledge.

Tham, H. (1995) 'From treatment to just deserts in a changing welfare state', in A. Snare (ed.) *Beware of Punishment: On the Utility and Futility of Criminal Law*, Oslo: Pax Forlag.

—— (2001) 'Law and order as a leftist project?: the case of Sweden', *Punishment and Society*, 3: 409–426.

—— (2005) 'Swedish Drug Policy and the Vision of the Good Society', *Journal of Scandinavian Studies in Criminology and Crime Prevention*, 6 (1): 57–73.

Thomas, T. (2005) *Sex Crime: Sex Offending and Society*, 2nd edn, Cullompton, UK: Willan Publishing.

Timonen, V. (2003), *Restructuring the Welfare State: Globalisation and Social Policy Reform in Finland and Sweden*, Cheltenham: Edward Elgar.

Tonry, M. (2004a) *Punishment and Politics: Evidence and Emulation in English Crime Control Policy*, Cullompton, UK: Willan Publishing.

—— (2004b) 'Why aren't German penal policy harsher and imprisonment rates higher?', *German Law Journal*, 5 (10): 1187–1206.

—— (2005) 'Why are Europe's crime rates falling?', *Criminology in Europe*, 5 (1): 8–11.

—— (2006) 'The prospects for institutionalization of restorative justice initiatives in Western countries', in I. Aertsen, T. Daems, and L. Roberts (eds) *Institutionalizing Restorative Justice*, Cullompton: Willan Publishing.

Transparency International (2005) *Transparency International Corruption Perceptions Index 2005*. Online. Available HTTP: http://ww1.transparency. org/cpi/2005/cpi2005_infocus.html (accessed 31 March 2006).

Tyler, T. and Boeckmann, R. (1997) 'Three strikes and you are out, but why? The psychology of public support for punishing rule breakers', *Law and Society Review*, 31: 237–265.

UMR Research Limited (2004) *Mood of the Nation Report: New Zealand 2004*, Wellington, NZ: UMR Research Limited.

United Nations (1971–2000) *Demographic Yearbook*, New York: Department of Economic and Social Affairs, Statistical Office, United Nations.

United States Census Bureau (1976) *Statistical Abstract of the United States 1975*. Washington: US Census Bureau.

—— (2001) *Statistical Abstract of the United States: 2000*, Washington: Government Printing Office.

—— (2005) *Statistical Abstract of the United States: 2004–5*, Washington: US Census Bureau.

United States Sentencing Commission (2005) *An Overview of the United States Sentencing Commission*. Online. Available HTTP: www.ussc.gov/ general.htm (accessed 1 April 2006).

Vachss, A. (1993) 'Sex predators can't be saved', *New York Times*, January 5: A15.

van Dijk, J. and Mayhew, P. (1993) *Criminal Victimization in the Industrialized World: Key findings of the 1989 and 1992 International Crime Surveys*, The Hague: Ministry of Justice, Department of Crime Prevention.

van Kesteren, J.N., Mayhew, P. and Nieuwbeerta, P. (2000) *Criminal Victimisation in Seventeen Industrialised Countries: Key-findings from the 2000 International Crime Victims Survey*, The Hague: Ministry of Justice, WODC.

van Swaaningen, R. (2005) 'Public safety and the management of fear', *Theoretical Criminology*, 9: 289–305.

von Goethe, W.J. (1797) *The Sorcerers Apprentice*. Online. Available HTTP: www.fln.vcu.edu/goethe/zauber_e3.html (accessed 23 May 2006).

von Hirsch, A. (1976) *Doing Justice*, New York: Hill and Wang.

—— (1993) *Censure and Sanctions*, Oxford: Clarendon Press.

von Hirsch, A. and Ashworth, A. (eds) (1998) *Principled Sentencing: Readings on Theory and Policy*, Oxford: Hart Publishing.

von Hirsch, A., Knapp, K. and Tonry, M. (1987) *The Sentencing Commission and its Guidelines*, Boston: Northeastern University Press.

von Hofer, H. (2003) 'Prison populations as political constructs: the case of Finland, Holland and Sweden', *Journal of Scandinavian Studies in Criminology and Crime Prevention*, 4 (1): 21–38.

Wacquant, L. (2004) 'Penal truth comes to Europe: think tanks and the "Washington consensus" on crime and punishment', in G. Gilligan and J. Pratt (eds) *Crime, Truth, and Justice: Official Inquiry, Discourse, Knowledge*, Portland: Willan Publishing.

Ward, I. (2001) 'Talkback radio and Australian politics', paper presented at the 43rd Annual Australian Political Studies Association's (APSA) conference, Brisbane, September 2001.

Williams, P. and Dickinson, J. (1993) 'Fear of crime: read all about it? the relationship between newspaper crime reporting and fear of crime', *British Journal of Criminology*, 33: 33–53.

Wilson, R. (2003) 'Portrait of a profession revisited', *Public Administration*, 81: 365–378.

Windlesham, D. (1998) *Politics, Punishment and Populism*, New York: Oxford University Press.

Worcester, R. (2003) *Whom Do We Trust? Neither Politicians Nor Journalists!* Online. Available HTTP: www.mori.com/publications/rmw/whomdo wetrust.shtml (accessed 8 May 2006).

World Economic Forum (2003) *Declining Public Trust Foremost a Leadership Problem*, Online. Available HTTP: www.weforum.org/site/home public.nsf/Content/Declining+Public+Trust+Foremost+a+Leadership+ Problem (accessed 23 May).

Wright, K.N. (1985) *The Great American Crime Myth*, Westport, CT: Greenwood Press.

Yearbook of the Commonwealth of Australia (1962) Government Printer: Canberra.

—— (2003) Government Printer: Canberra.

Young, A. (1996) *Imagining Crime: Textual Outlaws and Criminal Conversations*, London: Thousand Oaks.

Young, J. (1999) *The Exclusive Society: Social Exclusion, Crime and Difference in Late Modernity*, London: Sage.

Zedner, L. (1995) 'In pursuit of the vernacular: comparing law and order discourse in Britain and Germany', *Social and Legal Studies*, 4: 517–534.

Zimring, F. (1996) 'Populism, democratic government, and the decline of expert authority', *Pacific Law Journal*, 28: 243–256.

—— (1999) '1990s assault on juvenile justice: notes from an ideological battleground', *Federal Sentencing Reporter*, 11: 260–261.

—— (2005) *American Juvenile Justice*, Oxford: Oxford University Press.

Zimring, F. and Johnson, D. (2006) 'Public Opinion and governance of punishment: democratic political systems', in S. Karstedt and G. LaFree (eds) *Democracy, Crime and Justice, Annals of the American Academy of Political and Social Science*. (in press).

CASES CITED

Connecticut Department of Public Safety v Doe 538 US 11 [2003]

Ewing v California 538 US 11 [2003]

Kansas v Hendricks 521 US 346 [1997]

Muir v The Queen [2004] HCA 21

R v Bailey [1988] 10 Cr App R (S) 231

R v Queen [1981] 3 Cr App R (S) 245

R v Secretary of State for the Home Department, ex parte Allen [2000] 144 SJLB 152

R v Secretary of State for the Home Department, ex parte Doody [1994] 1 AC 531

R v Secretary of State for the Home Department, ex parte Hindley [2001] 1 AC 410

Taunoa v Attorney-General [2004] 7 HRNZ 379

Wynne v United Kingdom [1994] 11 HRL 61, European Court of Human Rights (18 July 1994)

INDEX